Frontier
Forts & Posts
of the Hudson's Bay Company

Fort Grahame - 1908 British Columbia Archives

hancock

house

by Kenneth E. Perry

ISBN 0-88839-598-1
EAN 9780888395986
Copyright © 2006 Kenneth E. Perry

Printed in Indonesia — TK

Production: Laura Michaels, Rick Groenheyde
Cover: Rick Groenheyde

Cataloging in Publication Data

Perry, K. E. (Kenneth Edwin), 1943-

    Frontier forts and posts / Kenneth E. Perry.

ISBN 0-88839-598-1

  1. Trading posts — Northwest, Pacific — History.

  2. Fur trade — Northwest, Pacific — History.

  3. Land settlement — Northwest, Pacific — History.

  4. Northwest, Pacific — History. I. Title.

FC3207.P47 2006   979.5   C2005-906715-2

Published simultaneously in Canada and the United States by

HANCOCK HOUSE PUBLISHERS LTD.
19313 Zero Avenue, Surrey, B.C., Canada V3S 9R9
(604) 538-1114 Fax (604) 538-2262

HANCOCK HOUSE PUBLISHERS
1431 Harrison Avenue, Blaine, WA, U.S.A. 98230-5005
(604) 538-1114 Fax (604) 538-2262

Website: www.hancockhouse.com *Email:* sales@hancockhouse.com

Table of Contents

Dedication

This book is dedicated to the entrepreneurial spirit of the men in the Company of Adventurers of England into Hudson's Bay and beyond, and to the Aboriginal people for their guidance and wilderness skills that essentially formed the backbone of the fur trade.

Acknowledgments

It is indeed a great pleasure to acknowledge the many organizations and numerous individuals who helped to establish this historical study of an almost-forgotten era. Thanks also for all the wonderful photo images, sketches and maps that were supplied by several of these organizations and were, in the end, combined into a single reference work for the generations of these times and generations yet to come.

Special thanks to the Canadian National Archives of Canada; B.C. Archives of British Columbia; Beinecke Rare Books and Manuscripts Library, Yale University, New Haven, Connecticut; Hudson's Bay Company Archives; Archives of Manitoba, Canada; Dr. John Lutz, University of Victoria, British Columbia; web page "Great Canadian Mysteries in Canadian History" David Hill-Turner, Curator; Nanaimo District Museum; Lionel Dallas, Okanagan Historical Society of British Columbia; University of Washington, Washington State; Heritage Branch of the B.C. Ministry of Aboriginal and Women's Services, British Columbia; Yukon Government–Historic Sites Program; Yukon Government–Cultural Services; Kamloops Museum & Archives, Jaryl McIsaac, Curator; Peter McIsaac of the Windermere District Historical Society, Invermere, British Columbia; and all the other great museums throughout Washington State, British Columbia, Yukon Territory and Alaska.

I also extend my sincere appreciation and gratitude to authors, historians and researchers at HBCA: Anne Morton and Pam Cormack, Murray Lundberg, Professor Pat MacDonald, Wallace M. Olson, Stephanie Flora, William J. Betts, Jean Webber, Richard T. Wright and Donald E. Waite.

I am especially grateful to my very good friend and amateur historian Helga Pennel for her relentless pursuits in digging out those hard to find reference materials and her overwhelming support and enthusiasm that aided so much to the overall success of this project.

My appreciation also goes out to the enthusiastic, hard-working "Dease Lake Gang" for their interest and time spent searching through the abandoned remains of Porter's Landing: Dan Stuart, Dave Harden, Ken Cook, Les Cook, Ken Perry Jr. and Blain.

Finally, a special thanks to my son Ken and my wife Carol for their editorial input and suggestions throughout the entire process of this enterprise.

Introduction

From the early 1800s through to the turn of the century several significant events unfolded throughout the Pacific Northwest and Western Arctic. Two of these events were: first, the fur trade era, and second, the gold rush period, with each event playing a major role in establishing settlements throughout the land.

This book attempts to present through photographs, sketches and maps the entrepreneurial spirit that reigned throughout a vibrant and exciting period of adventure and discovery. Most of the old structures were photographed somewhat intact with some, of course, more complete than others and some in a state of almost complete ruin.

That old familiar saying, "A picture is worth a thousand words," still holds true to this day. These images bring a special value in terms of clarity and understanding of the difficult times and life style that is not easy to express in words. The pictures presented in the following pages will hopefully evoke a certain reverence with the viewer of the fearless pursuits and accomplishments achieved by the major fur trading companies, their employees and Native peoples of the period.

There were essentially five major fur trade companies operating in the west: the Rocky Mountain Fur Company, Pacific Fur Company, Northwest Fur Company, the Russian American Fur Company and the Hudson's Bay Company.

The Rocky Mountain Fur Company (RMFC) conducted its operations mainly south of the forty-ninth parallel and was the last company to appear on the frontier. The RMFC was an American company that was organized in St. Louis in 1823 by Major Andrew Henry and General Ashley. Unlike the other fur trading companies, they did not establish forts or trading houses. Instead they employed independent trappers who essentially survived on their basic instincts and came up with their own shelter and food wherever they could find it. And all this occurred while defending their meager existence against wild animals and sometimes-hostile Natives. They were called Mountain Men.

Their system was simple; each summer the RMFC would establish a rendezvous point usually near a Hudson's Bay Company post in an effort to attract Indian trade away from their competitor. This ploy was surely met with a great deal of consternation and ill will by the "men of the Bay". Besides fur trading, the rendezvous provided a venue for the Mountain Men to relax, gamble, drink and dance — a party that would last for days if not weeks.

The Pacific Fur Company (PFC) on the other hand, operated much differently. Upon their arrival to the Columbia region they established the first trading post west of the Rockies in an attempt to take control over the whole American fur trade. This post was named Fort Astoria, after a wealthy New York fur merchant by the name of John Jacob Astor. Astor's fur trading activities east of the Rocky Mountains were well organized and quite successful; their next step towards expansion west of the mountains seemed obvious. However, as the threat of war between Great Britain and America grew in 1812, it was doubtful that the PFC could carry on business there without penalty. The company sold their fur trade interest to the North West Company, a Montreal-based enterprise.

The North West Company (NWC) a Canadian enterprise out of Quebec, was very rapidly taking over the west. This company was perhaps the only formidable fur trading company in the area, followed by the Hudson's Bay Company. In the early 1800s the NWC carried out an aggressive campaign to establish a trading network of forts across the western frontier that gave them an overwhelming lead in the trade. David Thompson, a former Hudson's Bay Company apprentice, joined the ranks of the NWC and in 1800 began his journey west to find the best overland route to the Pacific Ocean. Thompson crossed the Canadian Rockies through Howes Pass and discovered a great river, a river that was long sought after by Alexander McKenzie and Simon Fraser. That river was the Columbia. As he ventured downstream, mapping and surveying, he built several trading posts. By the summer of 1811, Thompson and his men reached the mouth of the Columbia and with much surprise found a place called Fort Astoria. A year later it was learned that the U.S. government was at war with the English.

The men of Fort Astoria were mainly British citizens in the employ of an American company and were, of course, unnerved by the circumstances with which they were faced. This event quickly set into motion a chain of events that ultimately caused the Pacific Fur Company to sell Fort Astoria and withdraw from the region. Shortly after their withdrawal, the fort's name was changed to Fort George. From this time on until the great amalgamation of 1821 between the North West Company and the Hudson's Bay Company, competition in the area virtually disappeared.

The Hudson's Bay Company (HBC) was established by Royal Charter in 1670 and its headquarters was in London. The Canadian operations in the early years were contained mainly in the Hudson's Bay region. Competition between the NWC and the HBC was fierce, both politically and in trade. The battles between them were settled in 1821 on a deed of partnership under the HBC banner, and this agreement gave the HBC a monopoly from coast to coast over the northern half of the North American continent. Fort George was abandoned in 1824 in favor of a new fort that was located approximately a hundred miles up the Columbia River and was officially dedicated Fort Vancouver.

By 1846, the much-disputed Old Oregon Territory was finally settled, and the border between Canada and the United States was established at the forty-ninth parallel. The Hudson's Bay Company withdrew from its Columbia River operations and re-established its western headquarters at Fort Victoria on Vancouver Island. During the Hudson's Bay Company monopoly south of the newly established border, it had conducted business with the Russian American Fur Company.

The Russian American Fur Company (RAFC) had for several decades carried out a fur trading enterprise mainly along the west coast. Their trading network of posts stretched as far south as Bodega Bay, California, and as far north as the Bering Sea. A small colony called Fort Ross was built in 1812 at Bodega Bay. It contained several buildings and was surrounded by a wooden palisade in a design that was typical to other fur trade forts along the coast. The hunting of sea otter was very lucrative for many years and brought high rewards in China; however, by 1820 the sea otter population was in decline. Fort Ross was mainly left with farming and stock raising, most of which was shipped to their Alaska trading posts to the north.

In 1839 the Hudson's Bay Company at Fort Vancouver and the Russian American Fur Company came to an agreement for the supply of food to Russian settlements in Alaska. Fort Ross was shortly after abandoned in 1841 when it reached an amicable agreement to sell its holdings to a private businessman at Sutter's Fort. A few years later the Russian Alaska territory was sold by the Russian government to the United States thereby relinquishing its rights in the North American continent.

These fur trading giants changed a wild frontier forever and the toughest and most shrewd of them all was the Hudson's Bay Company, which ended up controlling the entire fur trade network from coast to coast. These explorations left behind a legacy of historical names and structures reflective of a pioneering past. The majority of the forts, posts and dwelling places are now gone and have virtually disappeared back into the landscape with little or no evidence to be seen. Many of these old sites are today marked by cairns or memorials commemorating a time of a hard-lived past.

The prefixes "fort" or "post" by definition are quite different; the term fort is suggestive of a large structure with walls bordering its perimeter, whereas a post would suggest a more informal setting. Many forts were often styled similar to the great fortresses of Europe, but constructed somewhat differently. Most were built of wood instead of stone and were usually smaller in size. Most had high palisade walls, bastions and stockades to protect their trade goods, furs and personal possessions as well as to help ward off attacks from unwanted intruders. These fortified enclosures generally provided a reasonable measure of safety and security for its dwellings and their occupants. However, as time went on, the need for these elaborate and costly structures became less and less in demand.

For some reason that is not fully understood, the term "fort" was more widely used than that of "post". However, both designations were often used interchangeably for an establishment of the same place or region. Perhaps the designation fort was held in higher regard or prominence by those in charge at the time. By this inference it would suggest that a fort or a post were one and the same. This apparent anomaly certainly presents an interesting attitude of that era.

From these early frontier beginnings, cities, towns and small settlements evolved, some of which did not survive, while others flourished and now represent the place names we have come to know in our time as home. Names such as Fort Nelson, Fort St. John, Fort St. James, Fort Vancouver, Fort Spokane, Fort Wrangell and Fort Ross, to mention a few, have become a great legacy of an exciting past. During the fur trade and gold rush periods, forts and posts essentially became the main focal points for the exchange of goods and services. Many of those sites conducted successful business ventures lasting decades, while others were short lived due to various economic conditions within their particular regions.

The HBC, in its eminent wisdom, virtually planted a business operation everywhere there was an opportunity to turn a profit. The company adapted to change very quickly and moved often to meet the entrepreneurial spirit that prevailed for hundreds of years. The Hudson's Bay Company was an organization brought to a point of perfection in the face of immense challenge and in a wilderness far removed from any cultural or technical development. This company has survived the change of time and has remained to this very day a giant in the world of retail business.

Regardless of which trading company they worked for, the early explorers and traders essentially established the foundations and infrastructures for future generations to build upon. These wilderness frontiers are today known as Washington State, British Columbia, Yukon Territory and Alaska.

State of Washington

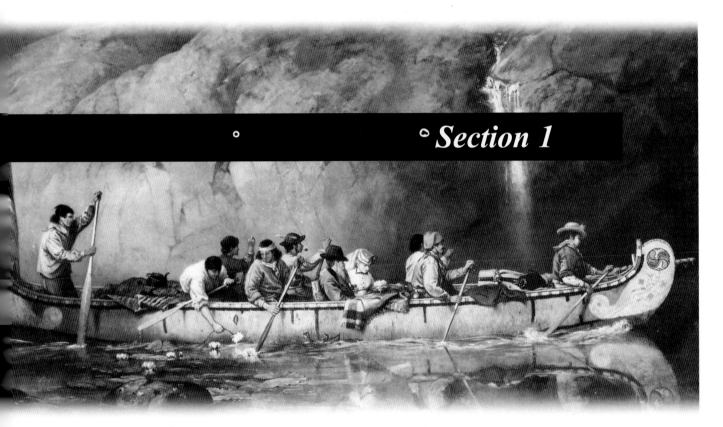

Section 1

Voyageurs and Native Guide *Oil Painting by Mrs. F.A. Hopkins, Hancock House Publishers Archives*

Washington State

Washington State is a land with coastal and inland mountain ranges that are perhaps unequaled anywhere in the northwest. Rugged high mountains dot the region with such a grand presence that they seemingly command a deep respect for the land. Mountains such as Mount Rainier, Mount Baker and Mount St. Helens rise up through a vast coniferous rainforest presenting spectacular vistas that can be seen from almost every part of the state. They are landmarks that are among the most magnificent peaks in the nation.

Winding through these stately mountain ranges is the mighty Columbia River, carving its way southward in an arc-like path toward the Pacific Ocean. This river literally became the main supply route for commerce in this part of the world. From the dense forestlands that cover much of the state to the semi-arid country of the southeastern region, Washington State, also known as the Evergreen State, has evolved into a very successful economic resource base for the United States.

During the early 1800s, the fur trade was the driving force in the region's economic prosperity. Companies like the Pacific Fur Company, North West Fur Company and the Hudson's Bay Company were the entrepreneurs of the day. Notable personalities like John Jacob Astor of the PFC, Dr. John McLoughlin of the HBC and explorer David Thompson were the stalwarts of the period. By 1821 Dr. John McLoughlin was pretty much the pre-eminent force in the region. Forts and posts such as Fort Colvile, Fort Okanogan, Fort Vancouver, Cowlitz Farm and Belle Vue Farm dotted the landscape. Small settlements evolved and life on the frontier, apart from the occasional Native uprising, was generally peaceful.

Between the years 1821 and 1845, settlers from all parts of the United States migrated across the great Oregon Trail to take up pioneer life on the frontier. This influx of settlers brought extreme pressures on the HBC and its fur trade, and even more pressure on the U.S. government — pressures that ultimately forced a negotiated settlement to establish a sovereign boundary that would close off a wild frontier that had been wide open since the beginning of time.

In 1846 an agreement was reached between Great Britain and the United States, and the border was established at the forty-ninth parallel. Shortly thereafter the HBC moved its Fort Vancouver headquarters on the Columbia River to their new headquarters at Fort Victoria on Vancouver Island. Company assets were sold to the United States.

The Evergreen State, a renowned stronghold of valuable resources that essentially evolved from the fur trade, is now a modern world-class provider of products and services to a global economy.

John Jacob Astor

Dr. John McLoughlin

Fort Colvile

Fort Colvile - Ca 1888 Northwest Museum of Arts & Culture
Eastern Washington State Historical Society, Spokane, Washington

Fort Colvile was named in honor of Andrew Colville, a member of the governing committee of the Hudson's Bay Company. The fort was located on the southeastern bank of the Columbia River a short distance up river from Kettle Falls. Fort Colvile was built by the HBC in 1825 to replace the old Spokane House, a North West Company post that had been a prime distribution center since 1810.

This fort was also considered the main receiving and distribution center for the annual "fur brigades" that originated from Fort Kamloops and other regions for many years. It was located on the main route between Fort Vancouver near the mouth of the Columbia River and Boat Encampment at Big Bend. It was also perhaps the most important site in the HBC supply line, as it served as a major rendezvous point and supply point for trade goods and food products for many years. During the later part of the 1860s and 1870s, Colvile's profitability had dwindled and the fort was closed ending a successful operation for the HBC that had lasted for more than four decades.

By 1941 the entire country surrounding the old fort disappeared forever into a watery grave as the Columbia River backed up behind the newly built Grand Coulee Dam thereby creating a lake 130 miles long. This body of water is known as Lake Roosevelt.

Lake Roosevelt looking North from St. Paul's Mission State Park. The farmlands and buildings of Fort Colvile lie under the waters, approximately center of the lake, just to the right of the large tree in the foreground.

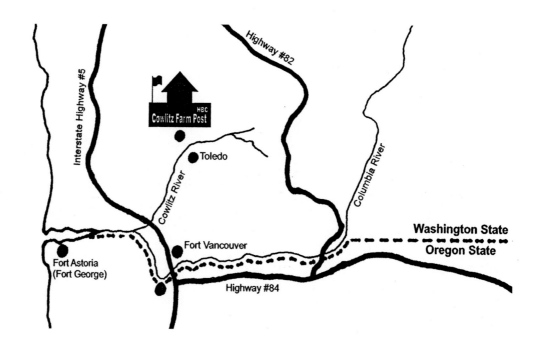

Cowlitz Farm Post

Cowlitz Farm was first established as a farm and settlement post in 1837. It supplied wheat for export to the Russian American Company, which operated fur-trading forts in Russia America known today as Alaska. The site was chosen at a previously established farm that was roughly developed in 1835 by two retired Canadian engages of the Hudson's Bay Company. Several new buildings were erected to help support a much larger enterprise. Besides growing wheat, the farm also raised cattle and other grazing animals.

The farm was located thirty-six miles due north of the Columbia River near the east end of Cowlitz Landing on the Cowlitz River that centered on a very large plain.
In 1841 John McLoughlin transferred the farm to the Puget Sound Agricultural Society, a subsidiary of the HBC. Cowlitz Farm closed in 1855 and was subsequently rented several years later, in 1859, to George Roberts. Roberts was a clerk on the farm between 1847 and 1851.

Fort George *(Fort Astoria)*

Captain Jonathon Thorne of the United States Navy and Commander of the ship *Tonquin* arrived at the mouth of the Columbia River on March 25, 1811. All hands were at once pressed into service to build a fort named Fort Astoria in honor of John Jacob Astor of the Pacific Fur Company. This early discovery essentially formed the basis of claim to the area and the final settlement of the Oregon boundary question that ultimately established the Canada–United States border in 1846.

The location of Fort Astoria was selected at a prominent rocky outcropping named Point George. By the time the fort was completed, Captain Thorne set sail on June 5 for northern waters on a trading venture. According to the ship's history, they arrived at Clayoquot Sound on the west coast of Vancouver Island. Months later a lone survivor of the ship arrived back at Astoria to report that all hands aboard ship were murdered by 200 to 300 Natives, apparently because the Captain had angered them through his heavy-handed diplomacy.

At midday on July 15, 1811, a large birch bark canoe supporting a British flag and eight voyageurs approached a small wharf just outside of the fort. First to step out of the canoe was David Thompson of the North West Company, their journey had taken them from the most upper regions of the Columbia River to the shores of the Pacific Ocean, ending a long sought-after inland waterway to the Pacific. Thompson would likely have arrived well before the Americans if it hadn't been for the desertion of several crewmen along the way that caused him to over-winter at the base of the Rocky Mountains. The outcome of the Oregon boundary dispute might have turned out differently.

After many financial losses throughout the PFC operations and the looming War of 1812 between Great Britain and the American government, Fort Astoria was acquired by the NWC, which gave it control over the entire country. Fort Astoria's name was changed to Fort George and later became the capital of Oregon Territory. Several large buildings were constructed, palisades erected and bastions strengthened. By 1821 the NWC and the Hudson's Bay Company had joined hands giving the HBC absolute dominance of the fur trade empire in all the lands west of the Rocky Mountains. Fort George was moved further up river a few years after the 1821 amalgamation, to a new location called Fort Vancouver. After 1821, many years of border wrangling went on until an agreement was finalized in 1846 that extended the border along the forty-ninth parallel to the Gulf of Georgia. A few years later, in 1849, the HBC moved its headquarters out of the Columbia region to Fort Victoria on Vancouver Island.

Fort George
National Archives of Canada

Fort Nez Perces

Fort Nez Perces - Ca 1870
Manuscript, Special Collections, University Archives Division, University of Washington Libraries

Fort Nez Perces was known by several other names during its history, Walla Walla, Willa Walla and Fort Walla Walla. Donald McKenzie and Alexander Ross of the North West Company established the fort at the confluence of the Walla Walla River and the Columbia River. The post was taken over in 1821 by the Hudson's Bay Company, keeping Ross on as manager until 1823.

According to HBC Archives in Manitoba, Canada, records described the fort as a mud fort. Fort Nez Perces was abandoned in 1855.

Fort Nisqually

Fort Nisqually - Ca 1940
Manuscript, Special Collections, University Archives Division, University of Washington Libraries

Besides being a fur trade establishment, Fort Nisqually was also a farm. Sheep, cattle and various crops were raised at this post. The products were sold or traded to Hudson's Bay Company forts in the Columbia District as well as to far-off places such as Russian America fur posts in the Russian Territory, today known as Alaska.

The fort was built close to the present-day community of Dupont. By the end of 1840 Fort Nisqually came under the management of the Puget Sound Agricultural

Company, a subsidiary company of the HBC. During the early 1800s the fort was often referred to as a Shepherds Station that was known by many names, such as Tlilthlow, Sastuk, Muck, Douglas Burn and Spanuch. However, the name Fort Nisqually prevailed. By 1846 the border treaty between British interest in the north and the American government became final. Soon after, the profitability of Fort Nisqually slowly fell into decline, fur returns from the region diminished and trade between the Americans became highly competitive. By this time new British trade routes were opened up north of the border, essentially establishing shorter transportation routes that were more economical to use and also alleviated the paying of local taxes and customs duties.

The general assets of the fort were disposed of by HBC clerk in charge, Edward Huggins, in May 1870, by public auction. This last transaction essentially brought this great HBC enterprise to a close, a business that lasted for nearly forty-seven years.

Today, Fort Nisqually is visited by many thousands of visitors annually at its new location in Point Defiance Park, Tacoma, Washington. Historic Fort Nisqually buildings were moved to the new site along with many other authentically recreated buildings. Together they present an historical memorial of a time that existed on one of Americas last frontiers — the Pacific Northwest.

Fort Okanogan

On their way to the northern reaches to the Okanagan Valley in 1811, David Stuart and Alexander Ross of the American Pacific Fur Company built a trading post. It was located on the Okanagan River approximately one-half mile upstream from the junction of the Columbia River. Stuart and Ross ventured farther up the valley finally ending up at a place called Kamloops by the local Natives, only to discover an area with great potential for fur trading. Trade was so successful with the Natives that they returned the following year to build the first fur trade fort in the area under the name Fort Kamloops.

Fort Okanogan - Ca 1812 *British Columbia Archives*

At the time of the War of 1812 the PFC sold its holdings to the North West Company, a Canadian company that was operating out of Montreal. By 1821 the NWC and the Hudson's Bay Company had joined forces under the management of the HBC. Shortly after the amalgamation, Fort Okanogan was moved a few miles farther upriver on the Columbia, apparently to provide a better vantage point to observe river traffic.

Fort Okanogan was regarded more as a horse station than as a fur trading post. Horse brigades of 300 horses or more would arrive each year carrying bales of furs from Fort Kamloops to this station. They were then loaded on boats destined for Fort George (Astoria), and in later years to Fort Vancouver. The last outfit (fur brigade) through Fort Okanogan was in 1847.

The Hudson's Bay Company maintained its interests at this site well into the 1860s. But little by little the fort fell into disrepair, and in 1894 a flood of great magnitude almost wiped out the fort in its entirety. In 1968 the final blow came when the waters rose up behind the Wells Dam, flooding the area and sending Fort Okanogan to a watery grave.

Fort Spokane

Fort Spokane, Site of Spokane House *Northwest Museum of Arts & Culture, Eastern Washington State Historical Society, Spokane, Washington*

Fort Spokane, also known as Spokane House, was located at Spokane Falls on the east side of Spokane River, about one mile above the Little Spokane River and ten miles northwest of the present-day city of Spokane. David Thompson recorded in his journal the longitude of 117 degrees 27 minutes, a measurement that was recalculated in more recent times as 117 degrees 33 minutes.

The North West Company, under the guidance of David Thompson, originally built this post in 1810. In 1812 the NWC purchased the competing Pacific Fur Company, which had established its post near Fort Spokane. The following year the NWC moved into the PFC establishment and by 1821 the Hudson's Bay Company had taken over all the NWC holdings through amalgamation. This post was updated to more suitable conditions to meet their future needs.

Five years later, on April 7, 1826, the HBC abandoned this facility for a more favorable location at Kettle Falls, which was to be named Fort Colvile.

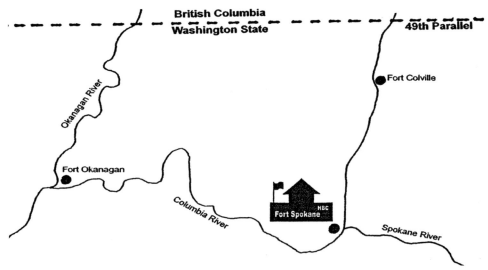

Fort Vancouver

Fort Vancouver - Ca 1860 *British Columbia Archives*

Chief Factor Dr. John McLoughlin realized that the location of Fort George (Astoria) would not be suitable for the main headquarters of the Hudson's Bay Company. McLoughlin set out in 1824 in search of a better location for the great emporium. His search took him nearly 100 miles up the Columbia River where he chose a site on the north bank approximately seven miles above the Willamette River; Fort Vancouver was built the following year. Five years later it was moved about a mile west to a plain above the riverbank, and the site in later years became known as Vancouver Barracks, a U.S. Army post.

By 1836 McLoughlin established a large farm consisting of 3,000 acres of fenced fields that produced grains, vegetables, horses, sheep, goats and swine. In addition he also built a dairy for butter and cheese, planted an apple and pear orchard, plus built two sawmills and two flour mills. This farm and fur enterprise brought annual return values to the HBC of $500,000 to $1 million to the company coffers.

The Fort maintained a twenty-five-foot containment wall of pickets (palisades) providing security for the apothecary shop, bakery, blacksmith, cooper's shop, trade offices for buying and selling, as well as many other retail shops. There were shops that sold woolen goods, clothes, ship chandlery, ironware and groceries of all sorts. Fort Vancouver was the headquarters of the Northwest/Columbia Department and New Caledonia as well.

US Army Post on the left and Fort Vancouver on the right

The original post was officially baptized on March 19, 1825 to commemorate the move from the old site of Fort George. By 1849 these headquarters were officially moved to Fort Victoria on Vancouver Island, an all-British territory, and by the spring of 1860 Fort Vancouver was abandoned.

Dr. John McLoughlin was chief factor at Fort Vancouver between 1825 and 1837 and again between 1839 and 1846. This highly regarded man was known by the local Natives as White Eagle; his hair was long, straight and pure white. He was also affectionately called by Americans and Europeans settlers as the Father of the Oregon Territory. Dr. John McLoughlin passed away at Oregon City in 1856 after twenty-two years of service to the Hudson's Bay Company.

Belle Vue Farm Post

Belle Vue Sheep Farm was situated on the banks of a stream in the center of a 1500-acre clear prairie, which was on the southeast coast of San Juan Island almost due south of Friday Harbor.

Besides a fishery being established near this end of the island in 1850, sheep were also raised as a primary source of food. James Douglas used the Hudson's Bay Company ships SS *Beaver* and the SS *Otter* to transport sheep from the farm to various forts along the coast. The vagueness of the Oregon Treaty regarding the specific location of the 1846 boundary dispute left the ownership of the island somewhat up in the air. It seems that in 1854 there was talk by the US Customs of seizing the HBC sheep. Douglas in his usual no-nonsense approach wrote to the chief trader in charge of the farm, Mr. Charles Griffin, to be ready for the collector should he come and to act with dignity and firmness of a British Magistrate.

In March of 1855 an armed party of American citizens landed on the island and demanded local taxes. Of course they were refused, and in retribution of this defiant posture the Americans carried off thirty-four rams. Over the years, tensions between both parties were raised on more than one occasion. By June of 1859 an American settler shot dead one of the HBC's most prized boars as it had trespassed on his land. This minor indiscretion set off what was later to be called the "Pig War."

Nearly five months later an agreement was reached by the British and the Americans to allow a military presence on the island. The Royal Marines established their camp on the south end of the island, now known as Garrison Bay, and the American military located their camp on the other end. Their occupation existed for twelve years. By 1861 the London Committee of the HBC recommended that the farm operation on San Juan Island be terminated when circumstances permitted. Sovereignty of the island was granted to the United States government in 1872 by Kaiser Wilhelm I, a German arbitrator.

Today the San Juan Island is a U.S. National Historic Park, and each year visitors to the island are treated to a very special event combining Canadians and Americans who don the military uniform of the period to celebrate the 1859 joint occupation of the island.

Belle Vue Farm Post - Ca 1859
The Beinecke Rare Book and Manuscript Library, Yale University

British Columbia
Canada

Hazelton Post - Ca 1911   *Kenneth N. Perry, Kelowna, British Columbia*

Section 2

British Columbia was one of the last frontiers of the Pacific Northwest with its immense landscape of rugged mountain ranges, highland plateaus, great lakes and river systems. A place with vast tracks of timber, precious metals and fur-bearing animals, there was seemingly an endless supply of virtually untouched resources waiting to be exploited for profit and personal gain.

By the late 1790s, Europeans came from the east seeking trade routes to the Pacific Ocean, while at the same time establishing forts and posts along the way in an effort to expand a vast fur-trading empire. Some of the earliest notable explorers were Alexander Mackenzie, the first white man west of the Canadian Rocky Mountains, followed by Simon Fraser many years later and David Thompson shortly thereafter.

These men were essentially responsible for mapping the country, establishing trails, portages and water routes throughout a land that was inhabited by Native Indians. This land became known by the fur traders as New Caledonia and Columbia River District.

Then in 1858 gold was discovered on Williams Creek in the Cariboo, setting off one of the biggest gold rush stampedes north of California. Men from all over the world came seeking their fortunes, fortunes that would be found by some and remain elusive to many others.

The fur trade continued into the early 1900s with only marginal returns from Native trappers. The availability of fur was getting scarcer as time went on. Long before the discovery of gold the Hudson's Bay Company had successfully gained control over the fur trade and for awhile their monopoly proved quite profitable. As the market for fur fell slowly into decline, the Hudson's Bay Company soon recognized that in order to sustain any type of business activity in the years to follow, they would have to redirect their attention and change their business strategy. This, of course, would require the establishment of new posts in areas where products of all sorts would be required. Mining towns and large populated centers were the places to be.

During this time the two British colonies, Fort Victoria on Vancouver Island and New Westminster on the mainland under the control of James Douglas and Amor De Cosmos respectively, were soon to be no longer. Both colonies were united under one provincial authority called British Columbia in 1866. New Westminster was for a short time the capital of the newly formed province until 1868 after which the capital was moved to Victoria; James Douglas became its first premier.

By 1846 the southern boundary between the United States of America and British interests to the north was officially established at the forty-ninth parallel. Road construction quickly began throughout the southern interior regions, stage coaches and freight wagons were soon driving north to the famous gold town of Barkerville and other centers of commerce, loaded with passengers and supplies. This new form of transportation brought to an end the great horse and mule pack trains that were the principle methods of freighting supplies to all points inland.

Honorable Donald Smith drove the Last Spike on November 7, 1885, at a small railway stop called Craigellachie commemorating the completion of the Canadian Pacific Railway, a transcontinental railway system that linked the country from coast to coast.

Alexander Mackenzie

Simon Fraser

The province also saw a new railway, the Grand Trunk Railway Company, being built to link the north country; it would be British Columbia's first railway. This change also brought about the demise of many paddlewheelers, the great flat-bottom boats that operated on rivers and lakes competing for profits and a hard-earned position in the transportation industry.

In July of 1871 British Columbia became an official province of Canada. Over a period of 100 years British Columbia expanded rapidly, ever changing and adapting to meet many challenges, largely as a result of the fur trade and gold rush eras.

David Thompson

James Douglas

Fort Yale - Ca 1860   *Hancock House Publishers Archives*

Fort Alexandria

Fort Alexandria - Ca 1914   *British Columbia Archives*

Fort Alexandria began its operation in 1821 as a fur trading supply depot that was located on the west side of the Fraser River just a short distance south of the community of Quesnel. The Fort became a central collection point for furs from the north country and the most northern starting point of the great horse brigades that transported the large eighty-pound bails of furs, two per horse, to Fort Colvile on the Columbia River.

In 1821 the North West Company built the post here as the northern terminus of their Pacific brigade trail. Goods that had been brought up the Columbia to Fort Okanagan were sent overland by pack train to this point, then distributed by water to posts of New Caledonia. The post was named for Sir Alexander Mackenzie who had explored the upper Fraser in 1793.

After the union of the NWC and HBC in 1821, Fort Alexandria was retained by the Hudson's Bay Company and played a key role in the logistics of the trade until road transportation supplanted the brigade in the 1860s.

By this time the Cariboo gold rush had slowly replaced fur-trading activities with more lucrative trade with miners heading north to the great gold fields of Barkerville. The Hudson's Bay Company purchased a restaurant and other buildings to operate a catering business on the east side of the river close to the Cariboo wagon road.

Fort Alexandria ceased general operations as a shipping point in June of 1867 and became a farm to supply produce to the fast-growing city of Quesnel and other areas. By this time the HBC had established a supply post in Quesnel that distributed produce from Fort Alexandria as well as other products to settlers of the region and passing miners.

In 1881 the HBC relinquished their property at Fort Alexandria, and by 1915 the old, decaying fort was pulled down and used for firewood, bringing an end to a once-thriving enterprise that was present for almost sixty years.

Fort Alexandria Cairn 2003

In 1821 the North West Company built a post here as the northern terminus of their Pacific brigade trail. Goods which had been brought up the Columbia to Fort Okanagan were sent overland by pack train to this point, then distributed by water to posts of New Caledonia. The post was named for Sir Alexandria Mackenzie who had explored the upper Fraser in 1793. After the union of the companies in 1821, Fort Alexandria was retained by the Hudson's Bay Company and played a key role in the logistics of the trade until road transportation supplanted the brigade in the 1860's.

Fort Babine

Fort Babine - Ca 1923 British Columbia Archives

Hudson's Bay Company Sloop

In 1822 Chief Trader (CT) William Brown arrived with thirteen men at Babine Lake to build a post. Brown chose a location near the point of land between the east and west arms, about eighty miles from the southeast end of the lake. The fort was originally named Fort Kilmaurs after Brown's parish of Kilmaurs in Ayrshire, Scotland. The post was abandoned in 1871 for a more favorable location situated at the north end of the west arm near the outlet of the lake.

The new location was selected because of its close proximity to the annual salmon run, which was an important dietary supplement for the fur traders of New Caledonia.

One hundred years after the building of the second fort, the Hudson's Bay Company closed its store on June 30, 1971.

Barkerville Post

***Main Street Barkerville -
Ca 1868*** *British Columbia
Archives*

Barkerville is a classic boomtown of the gold rush era. It is estimated that between 1862 and 1870 more than 100,000 people converged on the gold fields and this thriving town in the Cariboo. It was the largest town north of San Francisco.

By 1867 the Hudson's Bay Company opened up a store that was nothing more than a narrow shed annexed to a building that was formerly a drinking saloon. In September of 1868 the town completely burned to the ground except for one or two small buildings; fortunately for the HBC, the shed was saved from harm. Immediately after the event, the town was rebuilt.

In 1880 the HBC purchased a building and lot and conducted business from there for the next four years. Shortly thereafter they closed up shop and sold off their holdings.

Today Barkerville is a first class Provincial Heritage site and a world class tourist attraction. Thousands of visitors make their way each year to the famous gold fields of Barkerville, to experience firsthand what life was like here during this period.

Barkerville - Ca 1975 *British Columbia Archives*

Bella Coola Post

Bella Coola Post - Ca 1874   *British Columbia Archives*

On July 19, 1793, local First Nations people in the Bella Coola River area guided Alexander MacKenzie and his men down the Bella Coola River. As they were approaching what seemed to them to be the Pacific Ocean, MacKenzie could see a narrow inlet. Encouraged by what he saw, they set out the next day to find the open ocean. As they made their way along the narrow inlet they passed the site of what is now called Bella Coola. MacKenzie in his ongoing quest to see the ocean pressed on, navigating further westward through the long fiord.

After a short time the MacKenzie party came upon several Natives in canoes who seemingly were unfriendly and somewhat troublesome. Fearing for their lives, MacKenzie was forced to abandon his objective of reaching the open seas and returned quickly to the entrance of the Bella Coola River.

However, before leaving the area, this explorer and fur trader of the North West Company inscribed on a prominent rock face the words "Alex MacKenzie from Canada by land 22nd July 1793." The next day they left by the way they had come, retracing their steps back to the Blackwater River (West Road), up the Fraser River, Parsnip and Finlay Rivers arriving at Fort Forks on the Peace River-the place they had started from almost three and a half months previous. Alexander MacKenzie was the first European to find a route through the Rocky Mountains and beyond to the Pacific Ocean.

Natives at Bella Coola

More than seventy years after MacKenzie's arrival to the area in 1793, the Hudson's Bay Company established a fur trading post at Bella Coola. The post was sold many years later to a former employee, who continued a private operation into the early 1900s.

Black River Post

Black River Post was situated on the north side of the forks of the Black River (also known as Turnagain River), approximately seventy miles from its confluence with the Liard River, and about ninety-five miles southeast across country from Dease Lake. Its location was only accessible by pack train from Dease Lake.

The Hudson's Bay Company purchased the post from R. Sylvester in 1888 and operated it for many years under LaMountagne, the clerk in charge. In 1892 the HBC sold its interests to Mr. LaMountagne.

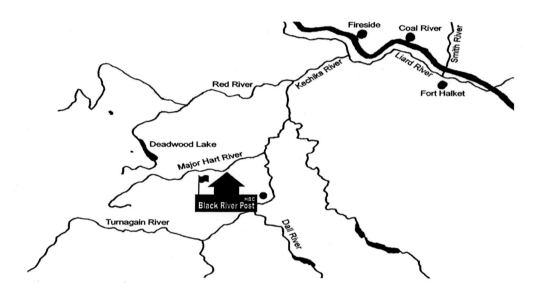

Fort Chilcotin

George McDougal from Fort Alexandria made a trip into the Chilcotin area in January of 1822 and described the region as abundant in furs. In July 1823, the Northern Council of the Hudson's Bay Company recommended that a post be built during the winter of 1823-24. But because of the mild winter and unrest by the Chilcotin Natives the post was put on hold. Finally on October 18, 1829, McDougal built a few cabins located at a small poplar stand at the confluence of the Chilcotin and the Chilko Rivers a short distance from Alexis Creek. Some trading activity was conducted during the following two winters. After several years of Native unrest in the area, the HBC abandoned their holdings in the later part of 1844; the post was moved to a more agreeable location at Lake Tluzcuz nearly seventy miles to the north.

Several attempts from 1861 to 1864 were made by the HBC as well as the colonial government to survey and build a road from Bute Inlet on the coast to Fort Alexandria in the east and beyond to the gold fields. Attempts had failed on several occasions. Apparently these repeated attempts were not well received by some Chilcotin Indians. Cultural differences, traditional land usage and the possibility of a mass invasion of newcomers likely played a major part in their destructive actions that eventually lead to a major confrontation.

Over a very short period between April and July of 1864, local Natives murdered nineteen white men, consisting of road builders, packers and settlers of the Chilcotin region. By mid-August of the same year, eight members of that war party attended a meeting near the old abandoned HBC fort on the Chilcotin and Chilko Rivers to discuss terms with the Governor. They were arrested and sent to Quesnel for trial and hanged about six weeks later.

The unrest in the region, often referred to as the Chilcotin War, was for the most part brought to an end by 1865 after the execution of one more Chilcotin Native at New Westminster, B.C.

Almost fifty-six years later, according to a sketch plan held at the HBC Archives in Manitoba, there may have been an attempt by the Hudson's Bay Company to pre-empt 99.5 acres of land on the north fork of the Chilcotin River in 1899 or 1900 near the Copeland's Ranch by the name of Fort Chilcotin.

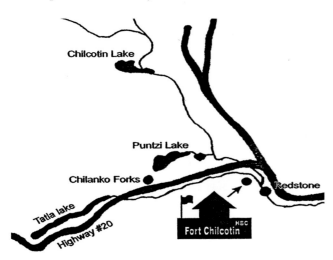

Fort Berens

Fort Berens was essentially a fort in name only; it was a small outpost under the direction of Fort Kamloops. This fort was named after Deputy Governor Henry Hulse Berens of the Hudson's Bay Company. It was a short-lived enterprise located on the east side of the Fraser River opposite the town of Lillooet, near today's modern highway bridge.

Construction started in February, 1859, and by May a log hut was evidently erected; however, by July 4 of the same year instructions were received by the factor at Kamloops to abandon any further work and have all materials returned to Fort Kamloops. A map sketched in 1859 by Lt. R. C. Mayne titled "Part of British Columbia" hangs today on a wall in the Lillooet Museum indicating the location of this fort.

By 1863 the town of Lillooet became an important center of commerce when an alternate route to the gold fields of the north country was completed. The overland trail from Port Douglas on the north end of Harrison Lake to Lillooet provided an easier route for thousands of miners heading to the Cariboo. Lillooet literally became a major transportation hub connecting traffic from the Harrison route to the Cariboo Wagon Road. Mile zero of the Cariboo Wagon Road began at Lillooet and ended up at the gold fields of Barkerville. The physical location of the old fort is fully developed now with buildings of all types conducting the business needs in the Lillooet area.

Fort Berens - Ca 1974 British Columbia Archives

General site area of Fort Berens, upper far left side of picture near the east bank of the Fraser River.

Fort Connolly

Fort Connolly - Ca 1911 *British Columbia Archives*

Fort Connolly was situated on the eastern side at the northern end of Bear Lake near its outlet to the Skeena River. The fort was named after William Connolly, chief factor in charge of the district. This establishment was essentially an outpost of Fort McLeod.

Samuel Black proposed to build a trading establishment in the area with the Sekani in 1824; the fort was never built. Two years later James Douglas was sent to the region to once again discuss the possibilities of setting up a post here. According to George Simpson, governor of the western district, the fort was finally built in 1827 with James Douglas in charge. By 1834, fur returns fell off after the building of Fort Halket to the north.

Fort Connolly was abandoned in 1878 on account of a small number of Aboriginals residing in the area. However, the fort was re-opened in 1887 and subsequently closed in the summer of 1892.

Fort Dallas

The contracts to build Fort Dallas were awarded and the windows and doors ordered; Fort Dallas was well underway. By all accounts, it was going to be a great structure measuring twenty-one feet wide by fifty-one feet long. The plans provided for a large kitchen of 15' x 21' at one end complete with a huge back-to-back fireplace and connecting wall. The fireplace and wall separated a 21' x 21' grand triple-front windowed council room. At the opposite end of the building measuring 15' x 21' included a very large bedroom, a connecting closet and a double-swinging, front-entrance door set leading to the council room. It was indeed an impressive design.

However, that's all it was - a design. By the time the work was to begin, the Hudson's Bay Company project was terminated. The doors, windows and other items of interest were redirected to other projects in the district. The termination of this project seemingly coincided with the closure of Fort Berens at Lillooet.

Fort Dallas (Lytton) - Ca 1864 British Columbia Archives

The site for Fort Dallas was chosen a short distance south of the present day settlement of Lytton and west of an old trail. This trail as seen in the left picture not only became the route of the famous Collins telegraph line but also became the Trans Canada Highway by-passing the town all together.

Old Trans Canada Highway - Ca 2003

Dease Lake Post

Dease Lake Post - south end - Ca 1900s *Kenneth N. Perry, Kelowna, British Columbia*

Robert Campbell, HBC clerk, postmaster and explorer reached Dease Lake in the first part of July, 1838, and built his first fort on the northeastern shore of the lake. Upon the completion of the fort he hoisted the HBC flag and cut the words "Hudson's Bay Company" and the date on a tree, thus taking possession of that part of the country. But he soon abandoned the post after trouble with Natives.

The Dease Lake Post moved at least five times between 1837 and 1928. In 1875 the post was re-established at Laketon then moved again in 1906 to Porter's Landing just south of the outflow of Thibert Creek. The new post was built primarily to provide supplies to the Siwash Indians and the Thibert Creek trade. The post was eventually closed in August of 1945.

Dease Lake Post - south end 2004

Dease Lake Post took on many names over the years, names such as Dease's House, Laketon Post and Porter's Landing, most of which were adopted by the local inhabitants of the area.

Hudson's Bay Company Barge - Dease Lake

Fort Esquimalt

Fort Esquimalt - Ca 1868 *British Columbia Archives*

Esquimalt Harbor is located on the south coast of Vancouver Island approximately nine miles north-northwest of the present-day city of Victoria. Among other shipping interests, this harbor was also the site of Fort Esquimalt, which was originally established in 1850, presumably as a fur transfer warehouse and likely supply point for tall ships that regularly used the harbor.

Improvements to buildings and wharf were made in 1868 and a year later the Hudson's Bay Company operated a store there under manager William T. Livock, clerk in charge, from 1871-72. It is unclear how long this post remained in operation, since the majority of the fur trade business was conducted at Fort Victoria. On or about 1881, the harbor was essentially taken over by the Esquimalt Naval Station.

Today, this west coast harbor is home base for the Royal Canadian Navy.

Fort Fraser

Fort Fraser - Ca 1905 British Columbia Archives

In 1806 Simon Fraser of the North West Company established Fort Fraser on Fraser Lake (formerly named Matleh or Natleh). Sometime after 1807 the post was abandoned for an unknown period of time. In 1810 J. M. Quesnel was sent to Fraser Lake to re-establish the post. In October 1817, the post was consumed by fire.

As a result of the coalition with the NWC, the Hudson's Bay Company acquired the post in 1821. In 1825-26 the post was rebuilt, which included a bastion. By 1829 Fort Fraser boasted to be the most valuable enterprise in New Caledonia. Throughout the years it had its ups and downs, and by 1885 it once again closed its operations. However, in November 1887, it reopened and the following year a new store and schoolhouse were built.

Old Town of Fort Fraser

Information sign at old HBC Fort Fraser in Beaumont Provincial Park - 2004

Ten years later references were entered in the post journals about miners passing through on their way to the Klondike. By 1914, W. Bunting closed the fort for the last time. Fort Fraser had a history of closing and reopening over a period of nearly 104 years, certainly a testament to ever-changing times and the entrepreneurial spirit to survive and prosper.

The site of HBC Fort Fraser is now a provincial park called Beaumont Provincial Park and is located at the east end of Fraser Lake.

Northwestern view of Fraser Lake from site of old HBC Fort Fraser - 2004

Fort George

Fort George - Ca 1911 British Columbia Archives

1830 Hudson's Bay Company Fort location and docking port for paddle wheelers at South Fort George.

Simon Fraser of the North West Company built Fort George, otherwise known by local Natives as Chala-oo-Chak, in the fall of 1807. It was located at the confluence of the Nechako and Fraser Rivers. While only temporary, this post provided the opportunity for Fraser and his men to build new canoes that would allow them to continue downriver in their search for a route to the Pacific Ocean. The post was abandoned the following year.

By 1820 the fort was re-established for permanent trade, and in November of 1821 the post was turned over to the Hudson's Bay Company at time of amalgamation. A store was erected in 1823, then, when all was seemingly going well, Natives murdered two men at the fort. By the following spring this post was also abandoned.

During 1829-30, Fort George was again re-established and in 1891 the post was moved about a mile downriver from the mouth of the Nechako River. It was situated on the west bank of the Fraser River approximately at the present-day location of the Fraser - Fort George Museum.

Fort George closed its operations in 1915 ending a period of trade that essentially established the early beginnings of Prince George as a major center for the north country.

Modern built bastion - Ca 2004
Fraser Fort George Museum

Glenora Post

Glenora Post - Ca 1975   *British Columbia Archives*

Glenora Post was established in 1874 by A. Choquette. It was situated twelve mil;es down river from Telegraph Creek on the Stikine River. The post was moved from it's original site to Glenora and then again to Teslin Lake in 1898 largely due to mining activity in the Stikine River area.

By 1899 the Hudson's Bay Company built a store at Glenora and in 1901 - 1902, a second store was established at Telegraph Creek to challenge competitors there. In the spring of 1903 the store was closed, it was literally cut in half and moved by teams of horses to Telegraph Creek a more central area for business at that time.

Fort Grahame

Fort Grahame - Ca 1908   *British Columbia Archives*

Fort Grahame was located a few miles up from the Finlay Forks where the Parsnip, Finlay and Peace Rivers had once converged. This fort was established in the 1870s by the Hudson's Bay Company, which had played an important role in the area providing goods and services in exchange for furs, gold and other commodities.

This once-important establishment forever disappeared beneath a great body of water when the Bennett Dam was built. Demands for electrical power prompted the building of this huge power-generating hydro station.

The dam is located near Hudson's Hope, which was also the site of another HBC post. The body of water that backs-up behind the dam is called Williston Lake, the largest manmade lake in the province. During site preparation of the enormous reservoir, work crews established a base camp at the deserted site of Fort Grahame. By the late 1960s, the fort site was demolished bringing to an end a legacy of a great enterprise.

Swanell survey crew - Ca 1914

Fort Halket

The Hudson's Bay Company constructed at least three posts at various locations in this region over a four-year period. The first post was located on the west branch of the Liard River in 1829, essentially for the convenience of the Theckenie Tribe. In 1831 it was moved to Buffalo River, close to the Reindeer River near to the east branch of the Liard.

In 1833 the post was moved again, this time to the confluence of the Smith River on the north side of the Liard River. Fort Halket was abandoned in 1865 largely due to the Theckenies going to Fort Nelson and Fort de Liard to the northeast for trade, virtually bypassing Fort Halket.

Today the site of Fort Halket is designated a protected area by the Ministry of Water, Land and Air Protection and is located within the Smith River/Fort Halket Provincial Park. Besides camping, fishing and some boating activities, the park contains the spectacular Smith River Falls that cascade into a large pool almost forty feet below. A short walk along a foot trail gives access to the falls from the day-use area.

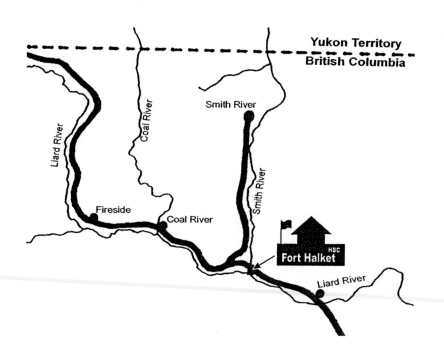

Smith River Falls - 2004

Hazelton Post

Hazelton Post - Ca 1911 *British Columbia Archives*

Hazelton Post was built in 1866 at Hagwilget close to Hazelton. The post closed two years later when trading became unprofitable. In 1880 the Hudson's Bay Company took over the premises of an independent operator that was located at the forks of the Skeena and Agwilget (Bulkley) Rivers.

By the fall of 1890, the post was situated on the south side of the Skeena River about one and a half miles from the junction of the Bulkley and Skeena Rivers. It became a major trading center for First Nations people and a supply depot for miners and the railway of the Omenica region.

Plaque, Hazelton Post - 2004

After 1900, Hazelton Post held the distinction of being a very important transportation hub for the distribution of goods and services to inland posts. In 1936 a massive flood washed away parts of the post; the post was subsequently moved to Government Street. However, after the completion of the railroad in 1914, the post had greatly diminished in value. It seems that the Hazelton Post maintained a presence in the area right up to 1970.

Today, one can take a walk through old Hazelton and visit many preserved historical buildings. Then visit the 'Ksan Historic Village, which displays seven traditional Gitksan longhouses and many totem poles, plus hundreds of Native artifacts in the First Nations Museum.

Hudson's Bay Company Post - Ca 1910

Hudson Hope Post

Hudson Hope Post - Ca 1906   *British Columbia Archives*

Also known as Rocky Mountain House and Rocky Mountain Portage, this post was founded by Simon Fraser in 1805 of the North West Company only to be abandoned some nine years later. Under the banner of the Hudson's Bay Company, Hudson Hope Post was moved three times during the years 1823 to 1913, the first of which was in 1823-24 to the south side of the Peace River at the east end of the Rocky Mountain Portage, then again in 1897 across the river on the north side, and once more to a new site on the north side of Peace River (date unknown).

Between 1865 and 1912 there were many attempts made by the HBC to establish a firm presence in the area. Unfortunately, their attempts were frustrated by a lack of trading activities, which made it difficult to hold on.

"Herbie" Taylor was post manager from 1905 to 1912. The town of Taylor, B.C. on the Alaska Highway was named after Herbie. In 1913 a new store was built, which included a post office for the growing presence of settlers to the area. By 1975 the Hudson Hope Post site was sold to the Hudson's Hope Historical Society for a museum.

Hudson's Bay Company Post - 2004

Storage cache on the Peace River - 2004

Fort Kamloops

Fort Kamloops - Ca 1865 British Columbia Archives

In November of 1812, David Stuart of the American Pacific Fur Trading Company built the first fur trade fort in the Kamloops area. Shortly after Stuart's arrival on the scene another notable company, the Montreal-based North West Company, built their fort under the direction of Joseph La Rocque. Competition was extremely keen in what was then a very lucrative fur market.

By 1813 the Pacific Fur Company sold their enterprise to the North West Company and returned to their original holdings at the mouth of the Columbia River. During this period the Hudson's Bay Company was forging ahead with their business ventures farther west and beyond the Rocky Mountains.

Fort Kamloops (Thompson Post) 2003. Old church in background, Kamloops Indian Reserve No. 1

Again, the drive to secure every fur possible throughout the land eventually led these two stalwart companies to join forces under the Hudson's Bay Company leadership. These changes ultimately resulted in the abandonment of some older forts for newer ones. In 1842, Chief Trader John Tod of Fort Kamloops chose to relocate their position to lower ground at the junction of the North and South Thompson Rivers. This newly built fort at the northwestern point of land had several buildings that were surrounded by high palisade walls, bastions and a large double-swinging front gate. Over the years, this location was plagued many times by flooding during the spring runoff, which caused a great deal of grief and anguish for its occupants.

Dissatisfied with the 1842 fort location on the north shore, Chief Trader Joseph William McKay decided to move the company's business. This time they moved to a place on the south shore about a third of a mile west of the present-day Overlander Bridge. Today this location is occupied by the Kamloops Municipal Maintenance Department.

By 1871 James McIntosh acquired a large parcel of land bordering the HBC property to the east side of its holdings for a new town site that ultimately brought into existence a fledging frontier village called West Kamloops.

Fort Kamloops - Ca 1846.. North shore location in the general area of Briar Avenue and Tranquille Road looking west.

Fort Kamloops Memorial Fort - BC Centennial. Officially opened July 20, 1966.

Kitwanga Post

Kitwanga Post - Ca 1947 British Columbia Archives

The Kitwanga railway station pictured here is believed to have been a Hudson's Bay Company post by the name of Kitwanga Post. On the large building in the background with a flagpole on the far side, the sign above the front door reads Hudson's Bay Company.

This post was abandoned and subsequently taken over as a railway depot. Today, all that remains of the building are a few boards and abandoned railway tracks. Unfortunately, a single totem pole is the only reminder of this once-important site.

The Kitwanga region is world famous for its totem poles, and one can be seen in the picture to the right side of the small building. Kitwanga is locally called Gitwangak.

Post remnants and totem pole - Ca 2004

Kootenay House Post

Kootenay House Post - Ca 1911
Windermere District Historical Society, Invermere, British Columbia

Kootenay House, also on occasion referred to as Fort Kootenai, was first established in the summer of 1807 by David Thompson, famous explorer, surveyor, astronomer and fur trader for the North West Company. Thompson built Kootenay House on what is known as Canterbury Point. The site was perhaps hastily chosen, as it was located on a windy bald point of land that protruded southward into Windermere Lake. This post was situated approximately two miles south of Toby Creek where it enters the Columbia River. By 1912 remains of burnt clay and stones were the only remnants visible; these stones were piled several feet apart and were apparently used as fire pits or a containment structure for fire. Apart from the stone piles, there was also evidence of there being at least sixty or seventy wooden posts inserted into the ground and standing on end about eighteen inches high. It seemed quite obvious to Mr. Basil G. Hamilton, a settler to the area, that these post were the remains of a palisade, a typical construction method of the period used to enclose an area around a building or other structures. This finding was confirmed by Reverend E. St. George Smythe, who had lived there in 1893.

Thompson abandoned his post just as it was near completion in favor of a more suitable location upriver on Toby Creek. Canterbury Point proved to be a difficult location in terms of packing food, water and other supplies up the steep banks. A second post was located a short distance up Toby Creek where it emptied into the Columbia River. This site was more suitable to Thompson and his men. It had better shelter from the wind, water was easier to access and, generally, it was a location that was easier to defend. Thompson was apparently besieged by the Piegan Indians for three weeks. David Thompson wintered there and then moved on downriver surveying and setting up other post along the way as he searched for the mouth of the river that entered the Pacific Ocean. The Toby Creek site was, for many years, a winter resting place for Thompson.

In 1922 a memorial fort was built by the Hudson's Bay Company and the Canadian Pacific Railway in David Thompson's name to commemorate the achievements of a great explorer and fur trader. The David Thompson Memorial Fort took on the form of a typical HBC fort complete with two bastions. This fort lasted only a couple of decades then fell slowly into decay. Subsequently, a memorial fort was built years later, only to be taken over eventually by the Invermere Golf and Country Club. The remaining mounds of fort debris were moved around, dug through and turned into a bunker. The golf course was a short-lived enterprise and closed about forty years ago, making way for new development. Canterbury Point is now referred to as Fort Point and supports a large residential community of luxurious houses that overlook Windermere Lake.

Kootenay House Cairn

Many artifacts and documents of the region can be seen at the Windermere Valley Museum in Invermere, a great source of historical records and memorabilia.

David Thompson Memorial Fort - Ca 1922

Kootenay House Post - Ca 1911

Fort Langley

Fort Langley - Ca 1862 *Kenneth E. Perry, Kamloops, British Columbia*

Chief Factor James McMillan originally established Fort Langley, which was named after Hudson's Bay Company London Committee member Thomas Langley. It was built at the junction of the Salmon and Fraser River, a place then called Derby. Besides conducting a fur trade business, the fort also established a salmon curing and agriculture operation.

On June 5, 1839, Fort Langley was moved farther upriver closer to Langley Farm. By this time an agreement was made with the Russian American Company to supply food products to their fur trade operations along the northern coastline. A year later the fort was burned to the ground but was quickly reconstructed.

By 1846 the International Boundary Treaty between the United States and the British government was settled. This agreement essentially closed down the horse brigade route through the Okanagan Valley to the Columbia River. A new route was quickly explored and developed through the Cascade Mountains to Fort Hope, making it closer to the Pacific Coast and less expensive to operate. Furs were then reloaded onto boats at Fort Hope destined to Fort Langley.

Twelve years later, in 1858, gold was discovered on the banks and sandbars of the Fraser Canyon setting off one of the biggest gold rushes north of the border. Fort Langley at the time conducted a thriving cash business exporting food to the Russians and now food and mining supplies to the miners. Within a few months gold seekers by the thousands invaded the country from all parts of the world, especially Americans from the south.

Due to fears of annexation by the Americans, on November 19, 1858, a proclamation was read at Fort Langley proclaiming James Douglas as Governor and Commander-in-Chief of Her Majesty's Colony of British Columbia and its Dependencies. This proclamation included all settled wild and unoccupied territories on the northwest coast of North America, commonly known as New Caledonia as well as adjacent islands. Basically, it claimed all the lands north of the 49th parallel, west of the Rocky Mountains, along the Pacific Coast Line and north as far as the Finlay branch of the Peace River.

The new proclamation in essence brought to a close the vast fur trade monopoly held by the Hudson's Bay Company and a new birth of a country called British Columbia. By this time competition for business throughout the newly proclaimed land was expanding at an enormous rate. New land transportation routes were being developed into the Cariboo; these routes ultimately by-passed Fort Langley leaving a once-prosperous business entity to slowly decline and, like so many other forts, it fell in disrepair.

Over the years from 1886 through to 1896 the Hudson's Bay Company conducted its business affairs at two close-by locations, one at Langley Post and the other at the Langley Saleshop. In 1896 the HBC operations at Langley closed, ending more than sixty-eight years of commerce in the region.

Commemorative Plaque
First Site - 2003

The original Fort Langley was built here in 1827, James McMillan in charge. It was the site of the first permanent settlement (later known as Derby) and the first soil cultivation in the lower Fraser Valley.

Looking north east from the north west bastion - 2003

View of the main house at the south end of the fort - 2003

Little Fort

Little Fort - 2004   *Kenneth E. Perry, Kamloops, British Columbia*

In 1850 Chief Trader Paul Fraser of Fort Kamloops established a remote trading post about sixty miles up the North River, now known as the North Thompson River. Due to the apparent abundance of furs available in the area, a post was built at the urging of the North River Indians. This small post was appropriately named Little Fort; it was essentially a small cabin located on the east side of the river under the management of Antoine Lampreau.

It seems that the fur returns from this post were not as originally expected. Two years later Little Fort was closed in favor of transporting furs and trade goods on a more frequent and less costly basis to and from Fort Kamloops.

Today, the small community of Little Fort survives as a reminder and legacy of what was once the location of a small Hudson's Bay Company post in the North Thompson region.

Information sign - 2004

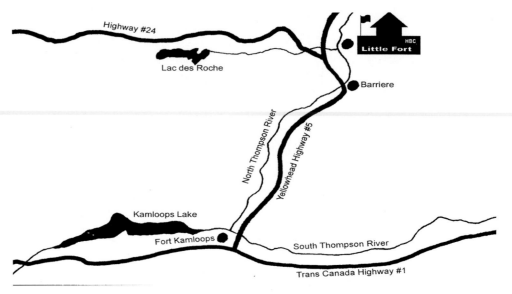

Lower Post

Lower Post - 2004
Hudson's Bay Company Archives, Archives of Manitoba, Winnipeg, Manitoba

In an area not too far from the present day Lower Post, in 1876 Rufus Sylvester operated a private trading post, otherwise known as a free trader By July 1888 the Hudson's Bay Company took over the post, which apparently did not do well A year later the post was closed and goods and equipment were moved to Liard Post.

Lower Post originally started out under the name Liard Post, which was located on the Liard River about one mile above the confluence of the Liard and Dease Rivers, and two and one-half miles south of the Yukon boundary, in British Columbia.

Forty years later, in 1940, the name Liard Post was changed to Lower Post. Nearly twenty years after that the post was closed, ending a trading enterprise of almost sixty-six years of service to the region.

Lower Post

Manson Creek Post

Manson Creek Post - Ca 1900s   *British Columbia Archives*

Manson Creek, a small gold mining community named after Hudson's Bay Company factor Donald Manson in charge of Fort St. James, is located approximately 150 miles due north of Fort St. James and about eighteen miles from Germansen Landing on the Omineca River. Somewhat overshadowed by the Great Barkerville Gold Rush of the 1860s and 1870s, Manson Creek was a site of gold mining activities in the early part of the 1870s. However, mining operations, regardless of location, generally face good and bad times associated with economic conditions beyond one's control.

By 1935–36, Manson Creek was once again in full swing — the good times were back. For the first time a large wood-fired steam shovel was brought in to boost production. It was at this time that the Hudson's Bay Company built and operated a store in the main settlement and provided miners with food and supplies. Oral history indicates that the store gradually failed due to poor economic conditions, largely as a result of mine closures caused by low water conditions.

The mines in the area still produce gold. The HBC store remains intact along with many other mining artifacts and buildings.

Manson Creek Post - 2002

McDame Creek Post

McDame Creek Post - Ca 1900s *British Columbia Archives*

McDame Creek Post, also known as Sylvester's Landing, was named in 1876 after Rufus Sylvester, when mining activity in the area was high. The post was located on the Dease River about seventy-five miles north of Dease Lake at the entrance of MaDame Creek. On July 1, 1888, the Hudson's Bay Company purchased Sylvester's Landing and conducted business there for about a year.

The post was moved twice, once in 1890 and again in 1928, each time trying to improve their business activities in the area. By June 30, 1943, the post was closed largely due to the company's inability to secure qualified staff to manage their business.

Abandoned HBC Trading Post - 2002

River view from post site - 2004

Fort McLeod

Fort McLeod - Ca 1906 *Hancock House Publishers Archives*

In the spring of 1805, the North West Company sent out an expedition west of the Rockies to a place they named McLeod Lake (previously known as Trout Lake). That fall Simon Fraser built Fort McLeod, the Nor'Westers' first post in the New Caledonia region, as a base to extend its operations west of the mountains. The post was specifically established to trade with the Sekani and various supply parties using the Peace River route to and from Athabasca. Fort McLeod was the first white settlement west of the Rocky Mountains. Sixteen years later the post was taken over by the Hudson's Bay Company through amalgamation.

According to an 1891 plan, Fort McLeod was located on the north end of McLeod Lake near its outlet. The post was relocated in 1853 to a new site about a half mile east on the opposite side of the lake. Presumable near the present-day store located at the side of the Hart Highway due north of Prince George. A commemorative cairn marks the site. This area is also the location of a large community of First Nations inhabitants.

Freight Bateau at Fort McLeod - Ca 1901   *Fort McLeod Cairn - 2003*

Fort McLoughlin

Established in 1834 by the Hudson's Bay Company, Fort McLoughlin was presumably named after Dr. John McLoughlin, chief factor in charge of the Columbia River District. It was a coastal post located on the eastward side of Campbell Island at Old Bella Bella also known as Waglisla.

After a short tenure of only nine years, Governor George Simpson decided that trade in the North Coast regions could be handled more economically by using the HBC SS *Beaver* rather than maintaining a costly manned post. In April or May of 1843, Simpson directed James Douglas to travel to Fort McLoughlin, close up their holdings and ship the men and whatever supplies and equipment on the *Beaver* and return to Fort Victoria (Camosun). Nothing remains of Fort McLoughlin today but the occasional references in published works or fur trade journals.

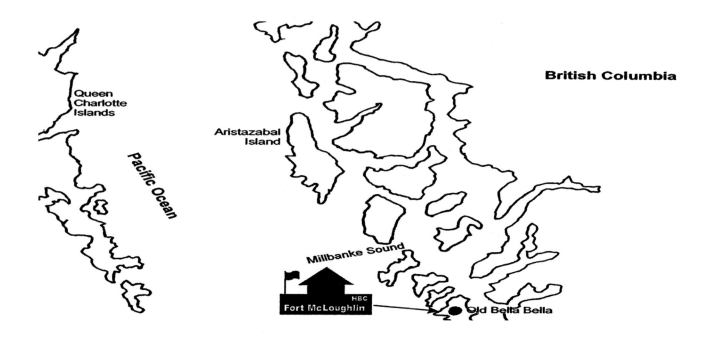

Nanaimo Post

Nanaimo Post - Ca 1862 *British Columbia Archives*

Nanaimo Post was at one time spelled Sne-my-mo and Nanymo. Surveyor J. D. Pemberton came up with the name Nanaimo after a First Nations community living in the area. The name was also thought to have been spelled Snuneymuxw, which when translated means "meeting place." However, prior to this name, in 1852 the settlement was originally called Colville Town after one of the HBC governors Andrew Colville. By 1860 the name was officially changed to Nanaimo. The post is located on the east side of Vancouver Island in a protected harbor by the same name.

Contrary to the usual fur trade activity associated with the HBC, coal was the prime trade product at Nanaimo. It was exported to California and other areas. In early 1853 James Douglas was instructed to begin purchase arrangements with the local Natives for Nanaimo. By the end of 1854 the purchase was finalized, and 688 blankets were exchanged.

The HBC brought miners and their families from Great Britain to work the coalfields as well as to fulfill its contract with the Crown to colonize Vancouver Island. By 1862 the coalfields were sold to Mr. James Nichol of the Vancouver Coal Mining and Land Company.

The post was comprised of a single bastion that was built in 1853 to protect the miners. It was a three-story, eight-sided square timber structure; the main floor was used as an office and store. It is believed that the bastion was also used as a jailhouse on occasion. Today, this heritage building is open to the public during the summer months, and each day during this period a cannon salute is fired at noon.

Hudson's Bay Company Ship SS Otter

Fort Nelson

Fort Nelson - Ca 1951 *British Columbia Archives*

George Keith of the North West Company founded Fort Nelson in 1805. It was considered a temporary store and was located about eighty miles up the Liard River from the forks. During the winter of 1812-13 the company employees were murdered and the post destroyed by the Beaver Indians. What provoked this action is unknown at this time.

By 1865 the Hudson's Bay Company established a new fort about 100 miles up the east branch of the Liard, which is now referred to as the Fort Nelson River. The post was built on the west bank at the confluence of the Fort Nelson and Muskwa Rivers.

Seventy-seven years later, in 1942, a newer post was established near the new Alaska Highway. The old fort was used as a trade camp and by 1944 it was moved about a mile further up river on the east bank. The new post by the Alaska Highway assumed the old name Fort Nelson, the old post was referred to then as Fort Nelson River; it finally closed in 1967.

Osoyoos Post

Osoyoos Post - Ca 2004   Kenneth E. Perry, Kamloops, British Columbia

The Osoyoos Post or House, as it was originally proposed, had a very short tenure. In March of 1867 it was located on the rise of land just to the west of the present-day bridge that crosses the narrows on Osoyoos Lake. Osoyoos was commonly known by the Aboriginal people of the area as Soyoos. For reasons unknown, this name was transformed over time into the present-day spelling, perhaps because of a misinterpretation in the way it was spoken by the Natives of the time.

Osoyoos House was a short eighteen-mile ride by horse from Fort Similkameen. Business seemingly did quite well for awhile providing the basic necessities of life. Liquor sales were also going well as was originally predicted by the post manager Mr. Theodore Kruger, according to a report written by Chief Factor Roderick Finlayson from Fort Victoria to the Board of Management of the Western Department. The profitability of this post was considered fair for a newly opened business. However, this post and the entire district were doomed when the Hudson's Bay Company decided to close the entire Similkameen District. This event coincided with the last horse brigade that came through in 1872.

Fur Trader Brigade

Perry Creek Post

Perry Creek is located a short distance northwest of Cranbrook and was discovered in 1876 by prospector Frank Perrier. Gold was found almost everywhere on the creek, which subsequently set-off a gold rush of some significance. This rush was second only to the Wild Horse discovery of 1863, which also brought a major stampede of gold seekers to the East Kootenay region.

A new town soon sprang up and was named by the miners in the area "Old Town." Why the name "Old Town" remains a mystery; perhaps it may have been due to the rapid development of camps and other mining infrastructures up and down the creek that may have held the threat of a newer town developing elsewhere on the creek. Machinery, waterwheels and tools of all sorts were pressed into service, even a steam shovel showed up on the creek. Perry Creek had become one of the best producers of gold in the East Kootenays.

Life on the creek for the average miner was more or less fairly stable for about a decade. Then almost as quickly as it began, the creek seemingly became depleted of its highly sought-after treasure and the rush ended. Old Town, a once-thriving community with its dance halls, saloons, hotels and other supporting amenities soon fell slowly into disrepair and was eventually abandoned.

Not unlike many other gold camps and towns of the period, the HBC-operated Perry Creek Post began selling equipment and supplies to the residents of Old Town and others passing through. Some opinions suggest that this HBC post may have only been an independent fur traders cabin, otherwise commonly known as a free trader. However, the picture titled Perry Creek Post suggests another.

Apparently, you can still find gold today in various sections of the creek especially near the falls area. All that is needed is a little bit of luck and a whole lot of patience.

Perry Creek Post *- Ca 1954* *British Columbia Archives*

Quesnel Post

Quesnel Post - Ca 1900s *British Columbia Archives*

Quesnel Post, also known as Quesnelle or Quesnellemouth, was named after Jules Maurice Quesnel. He was originally with explorer and fur trader Simon Fraser in the early years of discovery and exploration in the West.

The post was established in 1866 at the mouth of the Quesnel River to help recover losses sustained at the Hudson's Bay Company at Fort Alexandria. The following year it supplanted Alexandria as a supply depot to New Caledonia and surrounding area, and at that time newer premises were purchased from G. B. Wright.

In 1882 a new HBC store was built on the main north-south trail bordering the banks of the Fraser River. It was in operation until its sale to C. H. Allison in 1919, who then operated a drug store and post office there until 1949; in later years it was a coffee house.

Restoration of the building began in the early 1960s; today the log structure is maintained by the city of Quesnel.

Quesnel River

Hudson's Bay Company Store - 2003

Fort Rupert

Fort Rupert - Ca 1880s *British Columbia Archives*

Fort Rupert originally opened up in 1849 as a coal mine and headquarters for commercial coal mining. It was located on the northeast end of Vancouver Island at Beaver Harbor. Besides its coal mining activities, it also operated as a fur trade post. The post was named in honor of the first governor of the Hudson's Bay Company, Prince Rupert, Duke of Bavaria, Duke of Cumberland and Earl of Holderness.

The post mainly served as a coal supplier to the various steamships that plied the waters along the coast, among them were the HBC SS *Beaver* and the HBC SS *Otter*. William McNeil was the first chief trader to manage the post followed by many others over the thirty-three years the post was in operation. Fort Rupert closed its operations in 1882 and was sold to a free trader, which apparently remained in service well into the late 1960s.

Fort ruins - Ca 1929

Fort Shepherd

Fort Shepherd - Ca 1860 *British Columbia Archives*

Fort Shepherd, also known as Fort Pend d'Oreille, was built in 1856 on the west bank of the Columbia River across from the mouth of the Pend d'Oreille River, which emptied into the Columbia River. It was renamed Fort Shepherd after a governor of the Hudson's Bay Company. The fort was built at the urging of Sir George Simpson with specific instructions to locate the premises as close to Fort Colville as possible, which was also an HBC facility. This location turned out to be less than a mile north of the forty-ninth parallel and approximately thirteen miles south of the present-day city of Trail. The border had essentially separated the two forts, leaving Fort Shepherd on the north side in British territory and Fort Colvile on the south side in the United States of America.

James Douglas, chief factor at Fort Victoria, also urged that an all-British trade route be established as tighter controls on the newly recognized 1846 border were changing rapidly. The company wanted to avoid paying customs duties on trade goods and furs traveling north and south of the border. However, by the spring of 1870, the company realized that the Fort Shepherd region and Fort Colvile areas were no longer profitable. Fort Shepherd was closed by June of 1870.

The site today is apparently quite difficult to access. Should one visit the site, a stone cairn can be seen commemorating its historical significance. The cairn was placed there in 1959 by the Kinsmen Club of Trail.

Fort Shepherd Cairn - Ca 1959

Fort Simpson - Nass River

Fort Simpson - Ca 1862 *British Columbia Archives*

Fort Simpson was built in 1831 at the mouth of the Nass River under the direction of Peter Skeene Ogden and Aemilius Simpson to shut out the Americans from the area. The post was moved three years later to Point Maskelyne near Dundas Island south of the outer mouth of Portland Canal.

This post became the coastal trans-shipment point between Fort Vancouver on the Columbia and later Fort Victoria when other posts along the coast ceased operations. In 1859 Fort Simpson was refurbished presumably to meet the growing needs of the gold mining activities on the Queen Charlotte Islands. The requirements of the HBC operations at this location slowly fell into decline, and by 1895 they closed their doors.

Fort Simpson - Port Simpson

Fort Simpson (Port Simpson) - Ca 1900 *British Columbia Archives*

By 1895, changing times in the region were once again the stimulus to move, this time to the Tsimpsean Peninsula on the north shore of Port Simpson Harbor. This location established its position about forty miles between the mouth of the Skeena and Nass Rivers. Six years later, in 1901, the doors of this operation closed as all the other posts did, ending a period of rapid change that challenged the HBC management over a period of seventy years.

However, in 1934 the company once again re-established itself in the region, this time thirty miles north of present-day Prince Rupert in the Chatham Sound area. The newly resurrected Fort Simpson survived there for almost twenty years then finally closed its operations in June of 1954.

Port Simpson - Ca 1900 *British Columbia Archives*

Fort Similkameen

Fort Similkameen was named after the valley in which it was located and is a derivative word of the Similkameigh First Nations people of the area. There were two posts in this region during the latter part of the 1800s. The first post was built in 1860 by Francois Deschiquette located approximately in the center of the present-day community of Cawston. This post was also referred to by the local aboriginal people and some HBC factors as Keremeos, as noted in some historical post journals. Deschiquette's maintenance skills around the post were less than desirable; in fact they were by all accounts nonexistent. He was a very hard-nosed individual and did not get along with other people. He was apparently killed by Frank Petro during an argument.

Apart from the purposes of farming and trading, this HBC fort was also aware of the discovery of gold in the region and the huge potential that it might bring to the company coffers. The run-down state of the fort buildings gave the company cause to search out a new location in order to continue its business activities and hopefully prevail upon the good fortunes of the gold trade.

The demands on Mr. Roderick McLean, the newly appointed post manager for the new site, required a high level of business astuteness and trading shrewdness, a good foundation in the knowledge of farming and an accurate level of record keeping; the latter of which failed him. This second fort was located a short distance farther east down the valley on a large parcel of land that was better suited for the company's needs.

By the spring of 1867 business in the southern interior was at its lowest point ever. The 1860s gold rush had virtually collapsed and hard luck in the ranching community had caused huge setbacks. Horses and cattle were lost during severe winter conditions and the entire region was harshly affected. By 1871-72 the company was preparing to close Fort Similkameen, and in September of 1872 after the last outfit (horse brigade) came through, the fort was closed for good.

The land upon which the post was situated is now a heritage park and it contains the famous Barrington Price gristmill, located just west of the park property. This mill ground local grain for the purpose of making flour for the settlers and others who traveled through the area.

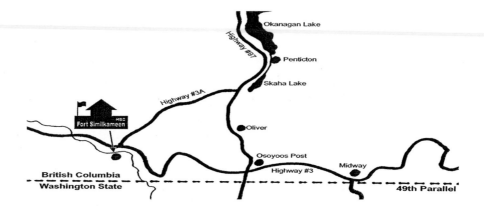

Fort St. John

Hudson's Bay Company Store - Ca 1948
Fort St. John - British Columbia Archives

The first fort built in the Fort St. John area was known as Rocky Mountain House. Construction of Rocky Mountain House began in 1794 and was located on the Peace River a short distance upriver from the mouth of the Moberly River. By 1805 the post was apparently abandoned; why this was remains unclear at this time. However, in the following year, the North West Company built a fort called Fort d'Epinette. This fort was situated about 500 yards downriver from the outflow of the Beatton River. In 1821, Fort d'Epinette was renamed Fort of St. John after the amalgamation with the Hudson's Bay Company. By 1823 the HBC suspended operations, likely due to poor fur returns from the area.

In 1860, nearly forty years after the closure of the old fort, a new Fort St. John was built. This time located on the south side of the Peace River, due south of the present-day community of Fort St. John. In 1872 this fort, like others before it, also closed its doors a seemingly characteristic trait reflecting the hardships associated with the business of the fur trade and the locations from where they conducted their enterprise. In the same year Francis Beaton, a factor for the HBC, relocated the post to yet another location. This time it moved directly north across the river from the previous fort. Shortly after construction of the new wagon road to Fort Nelson in 1925, the fort once again closed.

By this time the new wagon road was fully established and operational, the river road system ceased to be the avenue of choice as a transportation route.

Not including the present-day city of Fort St. John, there were five major fur trading forts and two free trader sites established and closed during a 180-year period. This is a remarkable testimony of business spirit in those early times. The persistent drive to maintain a business presence in the area also spurred on Factor Beaton to reopen yet another new fort on Fish Creek under the Hudson's Bay Company banner. It was located northwest of the last HBC fort along the new wagon trail to the north and near the modern community called Fort St. John. By 1975 the old HBC store on Fish Creek closed for good, bringing an end to a long business venture that served the region since the amalgamation with the NWC in 1821.

Fort St. John - Ca 1901

Fort St. James

Fort St. James - Ca 1920   *Hancock House Publishers Archives*

Fort St. James was originally established in 1806 and named Stewart Lake Post after John Stewart of the North West Company. Stuart and Simon Fraser had previously built Fort McLeod together in 1805 while on their way to find a better route to the Pacific. Stewart Lake Post became the headquarters of the New Caledonia District and ultimately the seat of government of all the lands north of Fort Kamloops.

By 1821 the Hudson's Bay Company acquired this post through amalgamation, and a short time later renamed the post Fort St. James after Chief Factor James Douglas. Douglas was apparently highly revered by the First Nations people in the area.

Among the dozens of post managers over a 170-year period, many of them took on senior positions with the HBC, managers such as Chief Factors William Connolly, Peter Warren Dease and Donald Manson to name but a few. All served the company with distinction.

Fort St. James was the main fur collection point for the north country. From this location, furs were transported downriver to Fort Alexandria on the Fraser for furtherance via horse brigade to Fort Kamloops and beyond to Fort Vancouver on the Columbia.

Fort St. James -
Ready to leave for
Fort Mcleod - Ca 1914

Fort St. James - 2003

Indian village at Fort St. James

Fort Stager

Site location of Fort Stage - top left corner at the junction of the Kispiox & Skeena Rivers
Fort Stager - 2004   Kenneth N. Perry, Kelowna, British Columbia

Fort Stager is believed to have been located in the Kispiox Valley a short distance due north of the community of Hazelton. The valley is bordered by two mountain ranges: Hazelton Mountains to the west and the Babine Ranges to the east. Local history places the fort at the confluence of the Kispiox and Skeena Rivers.

Kispiox is also the location of two Gitksan Indian villages, which proudly display a great variety of totem poles depicting Gitksan culture.

Information sign - 2004

Stoney Creek Post

Stoney Creek Post - Ca 1908 *British Columbia Archives*

Hudson's Bay Company post Stoney Creek was established east of Vanderhoof in 1886 to counter opposition that had been operating within the Indian village. Prior to this, the First Nations people had been trading at the HBC post at Fraser Lake.

During 1888-89, a trade store and dwelling house was built on the bank of Stoney Creek, a creek of about five miles long that connected Noolki and Tachic Lakes. This post was accessed by a trail about seventy-five miles due west of Fort George and about twenty-seven miles east of Fort Fraser at Fraser Lake. By 1892, fur returns from this area fell off and the post was closed.

Telegraph Creek

Telegraph Creek - Ca 1900 *British Columbia Archives*

Telegraph Creek was named after a Yukon telegraph work party that set out via this small creek that flowed into the Stikine River. Cla-ako-heen is the Native name for the creek; it was also known as Raspberry Creek by others. Telegraph Creek is located on the north bank of the Stikine River, 166 miles from its mouth on the Pacific Coast near Wrangell Island and twelve miles upriver from Glenora.

In 1901-02 the buildings and stock of the Casa Trading Company were purchased by the Hudson's Bay Company. By the winter of 1903-04, the HBC store at Glenora was dismantled; in fact, it was cut in half and moved by horse-drawn sleighs to Telegraph Creek. The Hudson's Bay Company operated a hotel/store combination, which was one of the largest buildings at Telegraph Creek. Apart from the fact this location was approximately the halfway point and repair center for the telegraph line, it was also an important embarkation point on the Stikine River to all areas of the Cassiar Region.

The HBC closed on August 16, 1972, and reopened as a private enterprise about five years later as the Stikine River Song Café, Lodge and General Store. Even though this former HBC post was built during the 1898 Yukon gold rush, it has been substantially upgraded to accommodate current-day travelers to the region.

Hudson's Bay Hotel - Ca 1943

Restored Hudson's Bay Company Post, now operating as a Stikine River Song B&B, Cafe & General Store.

Vernon Post

Vernon Post - Ca 1887   *British Columbia Archives*

Vernon Post at one time in its history was known as a main distribution center of cattle for the Okanagan Valley. The Frank Delory Ranch essentially controlled the entire area where the present-day city of Vernon is located.

In 1887 the Hudson's Bay Company opened up a store that was principally a fur-trading post and purveyor of supplies for the local ranchers in the district. Prior to this period, supplies had to come from Kamloops or from the coast by pack train, which took many weeks over very rugged mountain trails.

The Delory Ranch was purchased from Mr. Forbes G. Vernon in 1892 by the governor general of Canada, Lord Aberdeen. By this time, settlement of the region soon spawned many other enterprises, such as fruit growing and general farming of all types. Ten years later, in 1912, a second store was established that offered the new town of Vernon and the settlers of the region a wide variety of goods and services that varied greatly from its early beginnings.

By the 1920s, the fruit industry basically had supplanted the cattle industry and was transporting thousands of carloads of fruit by rail to markets throughout Canada and the United States. Today, logging, fruit growing, ranching and farming are the main resources of the area.

Fort Victoria

Fort Victoria - Ca 1858 *British Columbia Archives*

Fort Victoria was formerly known as Fort Camosun during the years 1843 to 1845. Camosun was a local Native word meaning "The Rush of Waters." As the ocean tide changed, it created a torrent of rushing water through a narrow rock channel located on the south side of the bay (this channel is now known as "The Gorge"). In 1845 the name was changed to Fort Albert in honor of the late Prince Consort. A few months later, in accordance with instructions from England, the name was changed again, this time to Fort Victoria after Queen Victoria.

This Hudson's Bay Company Fort was founded by James Douglas and J. McLoughlin who came from Fort Vancouver on the lower Columbia River. This fort was to function as a general depot for the Pacific trade. The fort was a square enclosure of 100 yards, surrounded by cedar palisades twenty feet high, two octagon-shaped bastions containing a half-dozen six-pounder iron cannons at the northeast and southwest angles. These bastions were built to ward off attacks from local Natives and other sea-going marauders.

SS** Beaver, **HBC ship off Fort Victoria - Ca 1846 *British Columbia Archives*

By 1849 the headquarters of the Columbia River District was transferred from Fort Vancouver to Fort Victoria. James Douglas was appointed chief trader, a position he held from 1849 through to 1852. From 1849 to 1859 Fort Victoria became headquarters for the British Crown Colony on Vancouver Island. By 1862 the city of Victoria that grew up around the fort was officially incorporated. In 1864 the old fort was demolished and the property sold off.

At the time of the gold discoveries on the lower Fraser River, Thompson River and Williams Creek in the Cariboo, the Crown Colony of British Columbia on the mainland was proclaimed at Fort Langley on November 19, 1858. In August, 1866, the union of both colonies, Vancouver Island and the mainland of British Columbia, took effect by an act passed by the Imperial Parliament of England. In July of 1871, British Columbia became the sixth province to join confederation with Victoria proclaimed as the capital city.

Fort Victoria *British Columbia Archives*

Fort Ware

Fort Ware - Ca 1939 *British Columbia Archives*

Fort Ware was named after William Ware; however, history seems to credit James Ware, his son the first postmaster and post manager. The post was located about one and a half miles above the White Water River on the Finlay River. According to Hudson's Bay Company records, it was moved many times over several years in an attempt to stay up with its opposition in the region. By 1927 the company had built a store, a few dwellings and a cache.

On March 13, 1938, it opened a post office to promote more business, however, a year later the post was closed due to a lack of sustainable business.

Wild Horse Creek Post

Wild Horse Creek

During the early discovery of gold on Stud Horse Creek in the east Kootenay region, there quickly began a sprawl of miner's tents, makeshift cabins and other structures along the banks of the creek. By 1865 thousands of men were arriving from every direction with the hopes of striking it rich. Stud Horse Creek was later renamed Wild Horse Creek at the urging of Edgar Dewdney; the name was thought to be more appropriate in light of the new trail that Dewdney was contracted to build. At the age of nineteen, a young man by the name of Jason Ovid Allard joined the Hudson's Bay Company. Jason was the son of Chief Trader Ovid Allard, a hard-working manager at many posts throughout the district. During Jason's early years, he helped his father run the HBC store at Fort Yale.

In 1866 Jason was posted to Wild Horse Creek. Very soon after his arrival he sold the entire store inventory to the miners; it was valued at $8,000. Young Allard figured that by the time he sent in his requisition for more supplies, they would not arrive at the creek before freeze up. Knowing that he was not authorized to make purchases of more than $250, he took the initiative and set out to meet an American pack train from Walla Walla, which he knew was making its way to Wild Horse Creek. Upon meeting up with the train some distance away, Jason quickly established a price of $23,000 for the entire outfit. Once back at the creek he promptly dispatched a bill to Victoria requesting payment.

*Panning the
Wild Horse Creek*

Outraged by Allard's expenditure, the Board of Management at Victoria immediately sent a representative and an official from England who was visiting at the time to investigate the matter. These two men were instructed to search down young Allard and reprimand him for his apparent disregard to company policy. When they arrived at Wild Horse Creek, Allard explained that all of his recently purchased supplies were sold at a tidy profit of 200 percent. Much to Allard's surprise, he was promoted on the spot and sent to manage Fort Shepherd. After a short stay there he was ordered to report to Fort Keremeos. Young Allard was not happy with his new orders, so he gave notice and left the company.

Jason Ovid Allard had spent all of his life to this point at Hudson's Bay Company facilities. He was essentially brought into the company, unofficially of course, on the day of his birth at Fort Langley. From that day forward his father tutored him in the ways of the company with profit being the driving force, and, to this end, he had more than exceeded the company's expectations while at Wild Horse Creek.

Westwold Post

Westwold Post - Ca 1944 *British Columbia Archives*

The beautiful valley of Westwold was originally known as The Frenchman's Prairie. The name Grande Prairie was eventually adopted in the early part of the 1800s. Apparently it was changed primarily to meet postal service address requirements, that is, an address that was not used anywhere else in Canada. For a very brief time the name Adelphi was used by some residents in the valley. It was a name that was synonymous with a local hotel in the area that was built in 1895 by Walter Homfray. The hotel also had a store, provided blacksmith services and, for a short time, served as a post office. Later the name Westwold was chosen mainly due to the name of the land the postal station was located on the West Wold. According to the English dictionary, the definition of the word "wold" means an upland plain or stretch of rolling land without woods.

Westwold is located about forty miles southeast of Kamloops on Highway 97. Little is known of this small Hudson's Bay Company post; it was presumably built to serve the great HBC fur brigades during the early part of the 1820s. The horse brigades or trains of 200 to 400 horses heavily loaded down with furs and trade goods made their way through this valley to and from Fort Colville, a major rendezvous site on the Columbia River. It was an annual event that occurred for decades.

The horse brigade system was developed to help shorten the distance from one fur collection point to another. This relatively new overland freighting system helped to reduce transportation costs significantly over the very slow and costly methods of river travel. For many years Grande Prairie was a prime territory for the pasturing and breeding of horses, a necessary supporting element for the brigade system that continued for many years. By 1848 the brigades had abandoned this trail in favor of a shorter route through the Fraser Canyon and in later years via the Tulameen country to Fort Hope. This was largely due to the changes brought about by the newly settled boundary between British Columbia and the United States along the forty-ninth parallel.

In 1864 Henry Ingram purchased the land the HBC post was situated on to start a ranch of his own. Ingram, a former miner and packer of the Cariboo region, had been involved in a new experiment using camels as pack animals during the early part of the gold rush. Quite abruptly this bold enterprise failed miserably. Apparently the rocky trails wreaked havoc with their hooves, not to mention the effect that it had on their ornery disposition, which often summoned a great dislike toward the beast by those who worked around them. Henry brought a few of these strange unwanted animals to his newly acquired holdings at Grand Prairie to assist him in land clearing. However, over time, most of these great ships of the desert were sold off. Many of them made their way to HBC post as tables meat. A few of these camels, however, survived right up to about 1889.

Like many forts or posts of the fur trade era, this post was also eventually deserted and left to decay. Henry Ingram passed away in 1879. He was buried on a hill above the land he worked on for many years. Both the large two-story house and the HBC post were eventually dismantled and cleared away, bringing an end to a great pioneering spirit that existed for several generations.

Fort Yale

Fort Yale - Ca 1860   *Hancock House Publishers Archives*

Fort Yale was situated at the head of navigation on the Fraser River in 1848 where the land and water routes met. This was due in part to the settlement of the Oregon border question and the end of the brigade trail from Fort Kamloops at that time. The newly established border essentially ended the Hudson's Bay Company operations in the Columbia River District and a new all-British route was needed. The Fort Hope site to the south was chosen. The Yale post was replaced as the main shipping point by Fort Hope when the overland route from Fort Kamloops to Fort Yale proved too treacherous. The trail through the Fraser Canyon brought huge loses in terms of furs and packhorses, so this route was quickly abandoned.

By 1850, Fort Hope became the focal point and center for gold seekers. But by the fall of 1858 Governor James Douglas ordered that town plans be made at Fort Yale, as it was fast becoming the jumping off point for gold seekers heading north.. Obviously, the last remaining original HBC building was not considered in the survey when the town began construction. This building by its very presence apparently blocked the passengers as they made their way from the paddlewheelers down Main Street especially during the height of the gold rush period; the building was finally dismantled.

To the left center of the above photograph a typical timber-framed warehouse appears to hide most of the new HBC store, showing only the top false front and rear of building; the old fort basically stood out like a sore thumb. It was eventually taken down to make way for departing passengers.

Five years later, the Cariboo Wagon Road between Fort Yale and Cook's Ferry to the north (now called Spence's Bridge) was nearing completion. Most traffic by this time bypassed Fort Yale as a stopover location for other points north along the way to the Cariboo gold fields. HBC operations at Fort Yale closed in 1892.

Front street, Yale - 2003
Trees on far right obscure the view of the river
banks on the Fraser River that were very open
during the 1860s and 1880s.

Original Fort Yale
Plaque - 2003
now hanging in
the local museum.

Yukon Territory
Canada

Section 3

The Yukon is a land that partly lies within the Arctic Circle, a land of many mountain ranges and large upland plateaus. The western part of the territory contains Mount Logan, Canada's highest mountain, which peaks at over 19,500 feet. As early as 1834, men of the Hudson's Bay Company had begun the fearless task of exploring the unknown rivers and valleys of this great wilderness land that lay north of the Peace River.

On July 19, 1834 Robert Campbell and a few men reached a beautiful lake that Campbell named Frances Lake in honor of Lady Simpson, the wife of Sir George Simpson. This period essentially established the beginning of the fur trade in the Yukon. From 1842 to 1848 Campbell built Frances Lake Post, Fort Pelly Banks and Fort Selkirk. This capable leader of men was a self-disciplined, well-organized and self-reliant individual, always ready to serve at the pleasure of his superiors.

Robert Campbell

Robert Campbell, chief factor, managed many trading posts and districts throughout his long and distinguished career of forty years. He retired from the company, married and had a large family after leaving the McKenzie District; he settled near Winnipeg, Manitoba, never to return to the Yukon. Campbell died in 1894. Unfortunately Campbell, like so many other names of the old fur traders who first discovered and followed the wild rivers of the west, is scarcely known today. The only outstanding reference to his name is a modern roadway called Campbell Highway, which runs from Watson Lake to Ross River along much of the route that Campbell and his voyagers took on their first trek into the Yukon.

Since the first discovery of gold, about 1869, mining became somewhat of a partner with the fur trade. However, it wasn't until the famous gold rush on the Klondike River in 1896 that mining became the most important economic source of income in that region of the country, basically superseding the fur trade as a primary source of industry. The Klondike rush touched off one of the biggest gold rushes since that in the Cariboo in British Columbia, some thirty years previous. Men came from every direction, some by the famous Chilcoot Pass and others by southeastern land routes. Their final destination was Dawson City, a city that sprang up virtually overnight. Thousands upon thousands of would-be miners converged on this location.

Gold was the commodity of the day; almost every piece of land was dug-up, turned over and processed for its precious shiny metal. The face of the land had taken on a new dimension and was changing fast as huge piles of stone heaped up in mounds could be seen for miles in almost every direction. Nearly fifty years later, other minerals took over the spotlight. Zinc, lead, copper and silver are now the Yukon's major mineral products.

The land of the midnight sun and Arctic lights, where fur trappers and gold seekers once worked undaunted in their pursuit of El Dorado, is gone forever. But the call of the wild still prevails in this land called the Yukon.

Frances Lake Post

Kenneth E. Perry, Kamloops, British Columbia

Hudson's Bay Company explorer and fur trader Robert Campbell was commissioned in February 1840, by Sir George Simpson to explore the northern reaches of the Liard River. On July 19 of the same year Campbell entered a beautiful lake, which he named Frances Lake after Lady Simpson, the wife of Sir George Simpson.

By 1842 Campbell established Fort Frances, the first of many HBC post in the Yukon. Nine years later, in the early part of 1851, the post was burned to the ground by disgruntled Natives.

Today, a modern highway stretching across the Yukon between Watson Lake and Ross River commemorates Robert Campbell's exploration of the region and is appropriately named Robert Campbell Highway.

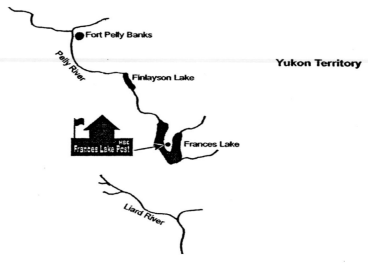

Herschel Island Post

Herschel Island Post - Ca 1928   *National Archives of Canada*

Herschel Island was named after Sir John Herschel, a British astronomer and chemist. In 1915 the Hudson's Bay Company established a residence and store on this Arctic Sea island. The store was built by Rudolph Johnston. By 1922 a new warehouse was built on Pauline Cove to serve a population of about 1,200 that wintered there, as well as for various ships that stopped by. After the collapse of the whaling market during the early 1900s, the local non-Native population declined to almost nil by 1964.

By the fall of 1937 and the spring of the following year, the buildings were locked up and the operation was moved to Shingle Point. The old store and offices were still standing in 1943; all other buildings were removed to Tuktuk.

In 1987 Herschel Island was established as the Yukon's first territorial park. It was created through the Inuvialuit land claims.

La Pierre's House

Kenneth E. Perry, Kamloops, British Columbia

La Pierre's House was named after a French Canadian Post Master. It was originally located on the right bank of the Bell River. It was moved at least four times to various locations between the years 1846 through to 1885.

This Hudson's Bay Company post was first built in the spring of 1846 and operated as a depot storage facility for both Fort Yukon and Rampart House. Edward McGillivray was the first manager in a long list of managers from 1846 to its abandonment in 1893.

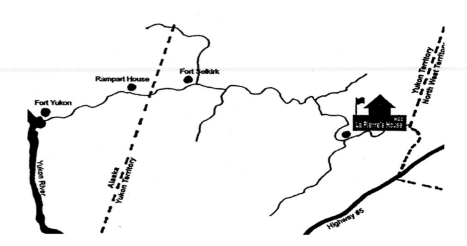

Fort Pelly Banks

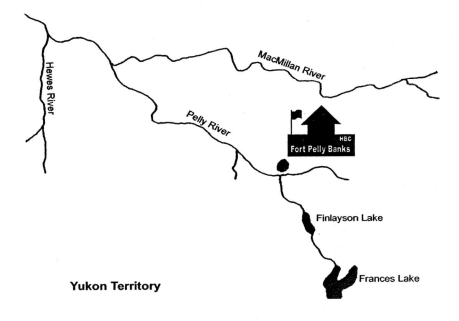

Towards the end of July 1840, Robert Campbell and his men arrived at the edge of a high, steep-sloped escarpment that bordered a river that was later named Pelly River. This escarpment was appropriately named Pelly's Bank in honor of Sir H. Pelly, an official of the Hudson's Bay Company. Six years later at the same location Campbell established Fort Pelly Banks. Campbell later learned that the Pelly River was in fact the Yukon River.

For years, the Pelly Banks post was plagued by a lack of adequate food and supplies from Fort Simpson. This apparent oversight essentially forced the men to live off the land, a task that was difficult at the best of times. The winter months were the toughest and more than once starvation came knocking at their door. Campbell complained bitterly about the situation but, seemingly, his complaints fell on deaf ears.

Several years later, in 1850, while returning from the far north Robert Campbell found the fort and the men to be in a deplorable state. Except for one house, the rest of the post was badly destroyed by fire, apparently by an accident. Once again, the men had been deprived of food and reduced to skin and bone. Their condition was appalling.

By late 1850, Chief Trader John Bell wrote to the governor and council that Fort Pelly Banks should be closed. It wasn't long after his recommendation that the post was abandoned.

Rampart House Post

Rampart House Post - Ca 1898 *Kenneth E. Perry, Kamloops, British Columbia*

Rampart House was built as a temporary post in 1870–71 at the foot of the upper ramparts on the Porcupine River. Its location was chosen by the Hudson's Bay Company because of the proximity to their other post Fort Yukon, which was located within the Untied States territory, when it was purchased in 1869 from the Russian Alaska Trading Company.

However, upon a new survey of the region, Rampart House was also found to be within American territory. Rampart House was also abandoned shortly thereafter. HBC employees and First Nations people moved to La Pierre's House farther to the east. The buildings were sold for $380 to a Church Missionary Society.

On July 23, 2001, at a historical ceremony held at the site of the remaining remnants of Rampart House, the government of the Yukon and the Vuntut Gwitchin First Nations signed a joint management restoration plan. The plan was essentially established to restore Rampart House and preserve a heritage site that represents the farthest western trading networks of the Hudson's Bay Company.

Teslin Lake Post

Teslin Lake Post - 2004

Teslin Lake Post was also known as Tackon Lake and TesLin Lake. In 1891 the Hudson's Bay Company began carving out a trail between Telegraph Creek and Teslin Lake. The new trail would allow pack trains to supply Teslin Post as well as provide a more direct route to the Yukon and other areas.

By 1898 the HBC claimed five lots on Second Street, Block 1, at Teslin City. In that same year, John C. Boyd built a store for the company with high hopes for a successful venture. Unfortunately, two years later the store was closed. The clerk in charge, Mr. George Adsit, was sent to Fort Liard (Lower Post).

Teslin Lake Bridge near Hudson's Bay Company Post site - 2004

Alaska
USA

Alaska

Alaska, the largest American state, occupies the upper northwesterly portion of the North American continent. It began its history on March 30, 1867, when it was purchased from the Russians for an approximate sum of $7 million. By 1912 Alaska became a United States territory.

However, prior to 1867 this land was principally controlled by the Russians and in which they operated a fur trading business for many decades. Primarily, they worked along the coastline, which included the Aleutian chain of islands and the entire most southern reaches of Alaska, adjacent to British Columbia.

The Russian American Fur Company established many forts on the coast, one being Fort Archangel Gabriel on Sitka Sound, which was the seat of government for that part of the world. After a victorious attack on the fort by the warring Tlingit tribe of the area and another successful attack in the Kake Strait, which resulted in the killing of all Russian men and officers of a Russian ship, the Russian traders quickly rebounded and brought about a penalty of immense control that ultimately suppressed

Fort Stikine (Fort Wrangell) - 1878 *Wrangell Museum, Alaska*

any further notions of aggression. In spite of the Native uprising, the RAFC established a new fort under the name Fort Archangel Michael. For a period of sixty-eight years the RAFC ruled Alaska.

By 1900 Alaska was known as the land of golden opportunity. Gold rushes one after another prompted thousands upon thousands of gold seekers on a course destined for Alaska. It was a period that lasted only a few years. Thirty-three years after the purchase of Alaska, statehood was officially bestowed on this rugged land making it the forty-ninth state in the Union. Its beauty abounds in every region; grand mountain ranges, narrow inland waterways and glaciers excite the imagination of any onlooker. Today Alaska stands with pride in its accomplishments and ability to supply petroleum products to markets south of the forty-ninth parallel.

The history of Alaska over the past 200 years has essentially been a blend of fur trading, gold mining and petroleum development. Old and new industry have slowly shaped the land into a modern infrastructure of cities and town that are second to none in the world of commerce - truly a land of golden opportunity.

Fort Durham

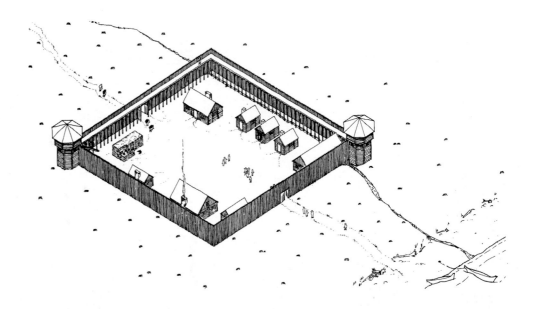

In June of 1840 James Douglas led an expedition by ship on the HBC steamboat SS *Beaver* along the northern coastline to search for a suitable place to build a trading post for the Company. Upon their arrival at the Taku River in the Russian American Territory, now Alaska, Douglas and crew met a friendly Tlingit Native who had approached their ship. After a few words Douglas invited the Tlingit on board. Douglas informed the Tlingit that they were looking for a suitable harbor to establish a trading post. The Tlingit pointed to the south and escorted Douglas and his men to an inland harbor.

On June 24 they arrived at the harbor then proceeded to unload their supplies and building equipment, and thus the building of Fort Durham began. Dr. John Kennedy was appointed factor and remained in charge of this post from its early beginnings through to its final closure in 1843.

Trade with the Natives was troublesome and difficult; they were very shrewd traders and were quite prepared to walk away from the trading process on more than one occasion. However, in the end trade was conducted but not without lengthy debates. The operations at Fort Durham were not as successful as anticipated. Fur returns were generally poor, the cost of trade was high and profits were low.

The fort was closed during the winter of 1842-43. James Douglas personally supervised the abandonment and had all the doors, windows and other items of value removed and loaded onboard ship. From that time on most of the coastal trade was conducted by ships of the HBC, which ultimately proved to be more economical than the high cost of operating forts along coastal waters.

Fort Stikine

Fort Stikine (Fort Wrangell) - Ca 1878 *Wrangell Museum, Alaska*

The Hudson's Bay Company in 1834 proposed to build a trading post about four miles from the mouth of the Stikine River. At the same time the Russian American Company was building Fort Wrangell, which was located on the northern tip of Wrangell Island a short distance adjacent to the mouth of the Stikine River. The island was named after Baron Ferdinand Von Wrangell, governor of the Russian American Fur Company.

In their attempt to establish a post on the Stikine River, which ran contrary to the British-Russian Treaty, the HBC found themselves quickly repelled by the Russians and were ordered to leave the area. Still eager to establish a fur trade presence in the region, the HBC pressed their case with the Russians until an agreement was reached. By February 6, 1839, the HBC signed a ten-year lease to operate Fort Wrangell. In June of 1840 James Douglas received possession of the fort, which he then promptly renamed Fort Stikine.

Native unrest in the area was widespread and trading was difficult throughout the lease period. A profitable position for the HBC was hard won from their trading partners. Frequently the Natives would leave the trading room if they thought they were not getting what they wanted or felt they were being short changed; tempers at times were high. The Natives murdered the son of Dr. John McLoughlin, chief factor of Fort Vancouver, who was clerk in charge of Fort Stikine during 1842–43, and unrest in the area prevailed for many years.

The Hudson's Bay Company terminated their operations and evacuated the fort in 1849. However, they continued to work the Stikine River region until the purchase of Alaska by the United States in 1867.

Fort Yukon

Fort Yukon, also known as Youcon or Youcan, was founded in 1847 on the Yukon River above the junction of the Porcupine River, sometimes referred to as the Rat River.

The fort was maintained as a base of operations west of the mountain range above the Yukon River. It was moved about one mile down river in 1864 and rebuilding started. Each time they moved, they believed they were in Yukon Territory. Two years after the United States purchased Alaska in 1867 the HBC was prompted to move once again. This time they moved about seventy miles up river to a place call Rampart House, which they believed was out of American territory.

Sometime after the move it was determined in a survey that Rampart House was also within American territory, so it, too, was abandoned. Trade with the Indians then moved to La Pierre's House, another HBC post, this time clearly in Yukon Territory. Fort Yukon was a fort that was virtually chased from one location to another until its final resting place at La Pierre's House.

Dawson City Museum and Historical Society, Yukon Territory